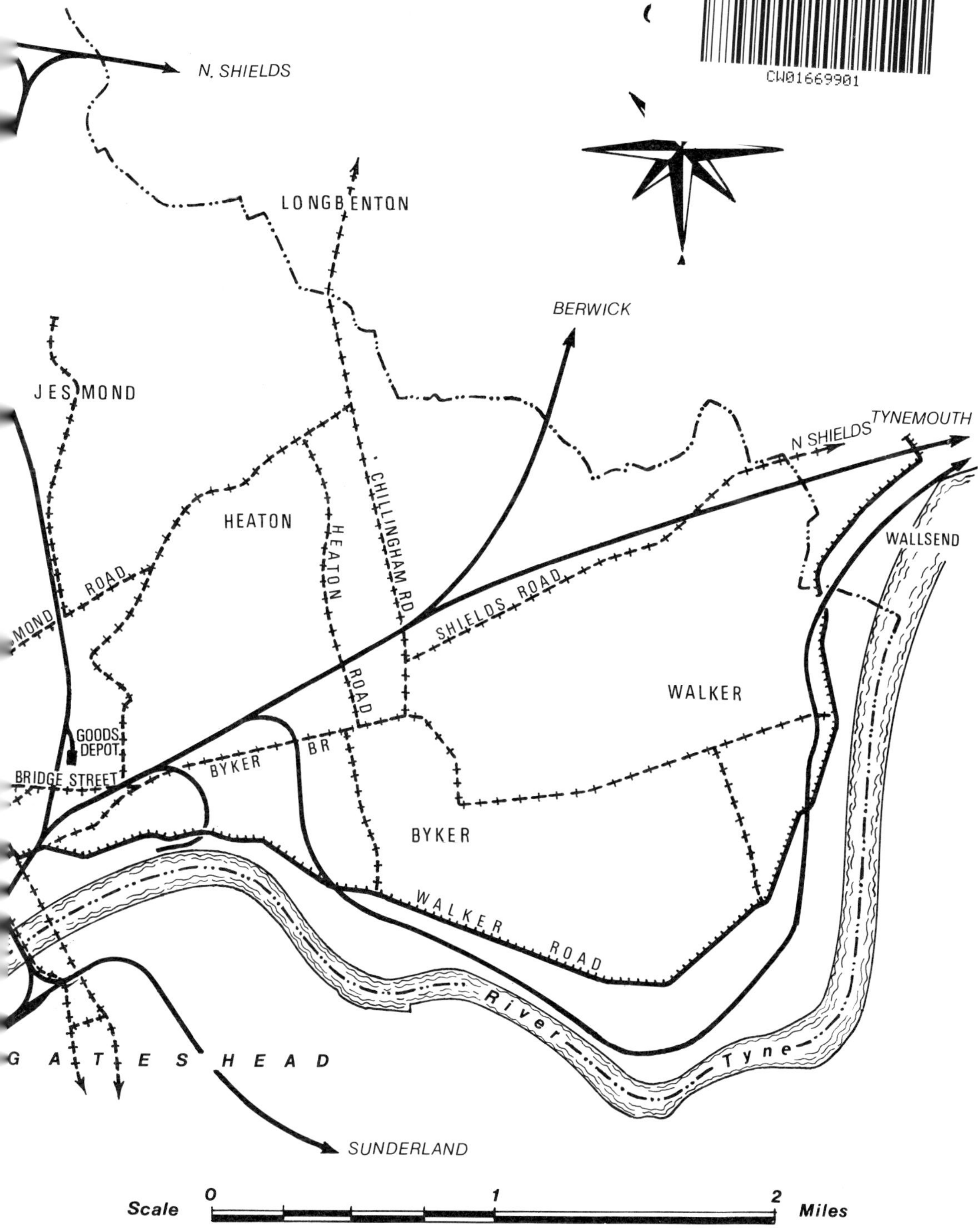

N. SHIELDS
LONGBENTON
BERWICK
JESMOND
TYNEMOUTH
N SHIELDS
HEATON
HEATON ROAD
CHILLINGHAM RD
WALLSEND
ROAD
MOND
SHIELDS ROAD
WALKER
GOODS DEPOT
BRIDGE STREET
BYKER BR
BYKER
WALKER ROAD
River Tyne
GATESHEAD
SUNDERLAND
Scale
0
1
2
Miles

In central Newcastle in 1939; coming in from Wallsend, trolleybus No 52 (a 1937 Metropolitan-Cammell-bodied Karrier E6A) uses the St Nicholas loop on its departure for the Fox & Hounds terminus on the Denton Burn route. Introduced in 1935, Newcastle's trolleybuses had already replaced many of the city's tramcars, but plans for operation over the Tyne into Gateshead never materialised. Standing alongside No 52 is a Morris Commercial van of Wallsend Co-operative Laundries. *Ian Allan Library*

Roads and Rails of TYNE and WEAR

1900~1980

J. Joyce

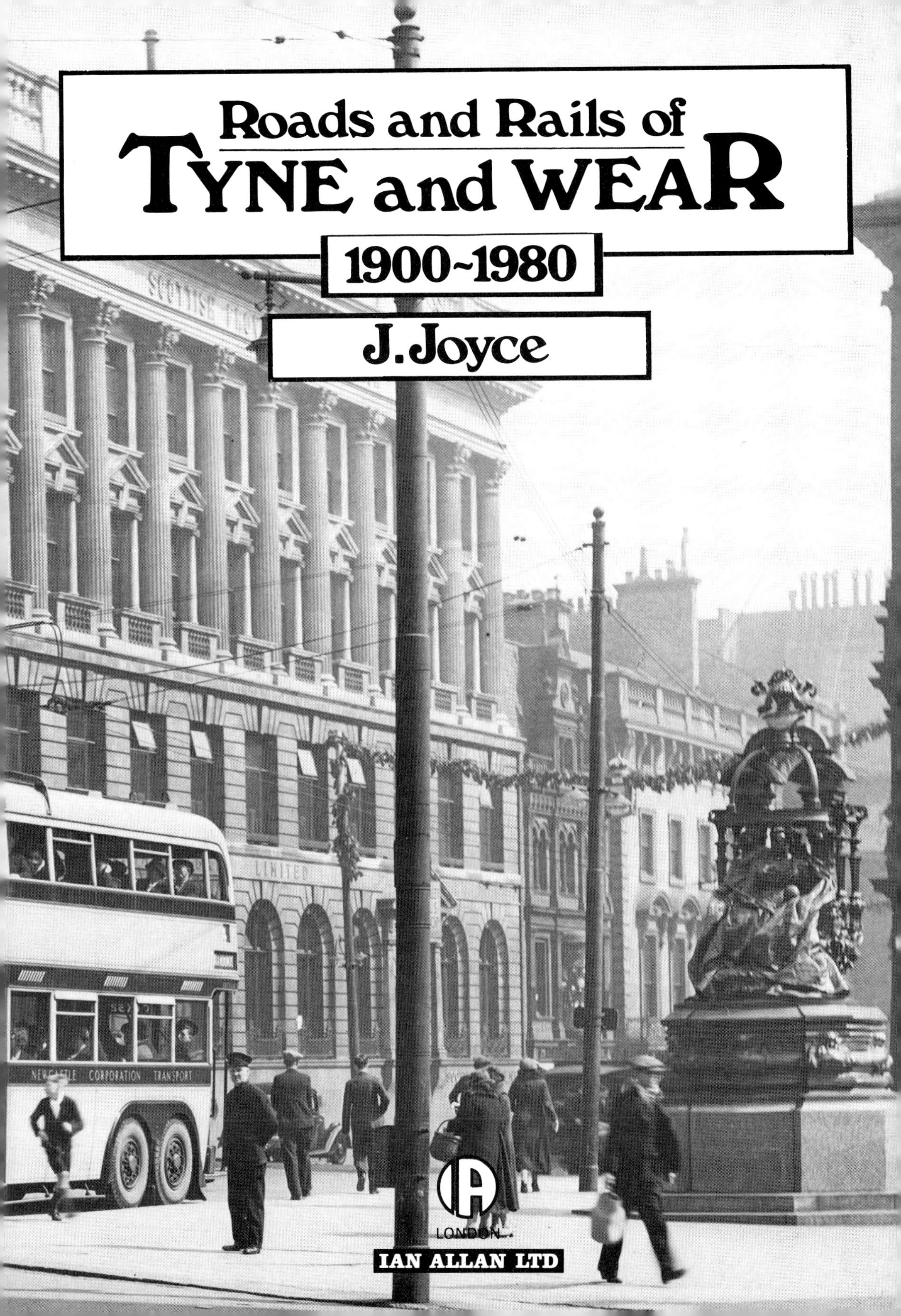

LONDON
IAN ALLAN LTD

Bibliography

Books

Allen, Cecil J.: *The North Eastern Railway,* Ian Allan Ltd, 1974.

Allen, Cecil J.: *The London & North Eastern Railway,* Ian Allan Ltd, 1966.

Bett, W. H., and Gillham, J. C., edited J. H. Price: *The Tramways of North East England,* Light Rail Transit Association, 1977.

Burrows, G.: *The Trolleybuses of South Shields,* Trolleybooks, 1976.

Canneaux, T. P., and Hanson, N. H.: *The Trolleybuses of Newcastle upon Tyne,* Trolleybooks, 1974.

Dunbar, Charles S.: *Twixt Wear and Tees,* Passenger Transport, 1954.

From Trams to Buses, Gateshead & District Omnibus Co, 1951.

Hearse, George S.; *The Tramways of Northumberland,* Author, 1961.

Hearse, George S.: *The Tramways of Gateshead,* Author, 1965.

Hearse, George S.: *The Tramways of Jarrow and South Shields,* Author, 1971.

Hearse, George S.: *Remember the Trams; Newcastle upon Tyne,* Author, 1978.

Hennessey, R. A. S.: *The Electric Railway that Never Was,* Oriel Press, 1970.

Hoole, K.: *The North Eastern Electrics,* Oakwood Press, 1961.

Horse Tram to Metro; 100 Years of Local Public Transport in Tyne & Wear, Tyne & Wear PTE, 1978.

MacLean, J. S.: *The Locomotives of the North Eastern Railway,* B. Robinson, Newcastle, 1905.

Staddon, S. A.: *The Tramways of Sunderland,* Advertiser Press, 1964.

The Tyneside Electrified Lines of the LNER, Railway Gazette, 1939.

Periodicals

Buses; The Engineer; Journal of the Institution of Municipal Engineers; Meccano Magazine; Modern Transport; Modern Tramway; Omnibus Magazine; Railway Gazette; Railway World; The Railway Magazine; Transport World; Tramway Review.

Contents

First published 1985

ISBN 0 7110 1472 8

Published by Ian Allan Ltd, Shepperton, Surrey; and printed by Ian Allan Printing Ltd at their works at Coombelands in Runnymede, England

Introduction

The place of the Tyne & Wear area in Britain's transport tradition is long established; it is only necessary to mention such names as George and Robert Stephenson and such locations as Wylam and Killingworth to recall its premier place in the evolution of the modern railway. Today the inheritance is maintained by the high-speed diesel trains which still cross Stephenson's great High Level bridge into Newcastle Central on the trunk East Coast route. But no less is the tradition upheld by the road and rail network of the Tyne & Wear Passenger Transport Executive, which operates Britain's unique Metro as part of its integrated bus and train system embracing not only Newcastle and Gateshead, but Tynemouth, North and South Shields and Sunderland as well as their extensive suburbs and hinterland.

Behind the present-day scene lies a period when local transit facilities underwent a transformation. During the first part of this century horse-drawn tramcars finally succumbed to the electric tramcar which brought a new age of rapid and convenient short-distance travel. Electric traction also revolutionised local railways: the North Eastern Railway was a pioneer in electrification. Then came the age of the motorbus and the private motor car, building on the established lines of communication but vastly extending their influence from local to regional and adding their own impact to the forces welding once separate communities on Tyneside and Wearside into one coherent region. But with this came further problems as traffic congestion demanded new road facilities and stimulated a new look at railed transport to alleviate the pressures of motorisation.

It is the purpose of this book to look back at Tyne & Wear's transport in the earlier years of this century: what facilities were there, what effects did they have, and how did they change over this period of time? It is hoped that the contemporary illustrations will depict something of this past era, while the quotations may serve to remind us of the problems facing our predecessors and what they thought about them. What was the purpose of a local transport system? How far should a municipal undertaking be a profit-making or a service organisation? What were the respective roles of road and rail? We may see something of the difficulties of integrating transport where different authorities with conflicting interests were involved. And overall stands the basic theme of transformation from local to regional; how from being a purely local interest, often jealously guarded against intruders, local transport in its numerous forms and under varied control evolved into the regional network of Tyne & Wear transport today.

For too much of our period this process was taking place against a sombre background of serious industrial depression, as the area's traditional staple industries of coal mining and shipbuilding were undergoing rapid decline, and inevitably this affected the demand for transport and its overall development. Nevertheless other forces were at work to bring new industries and new facilities, again affecting the transport pattern; the motorbus, for example, brought greater mobility for the worker seeking new employment, while new road projects (ironically often undertaken as unemployment relief) brought improved highways and easier road travel.

But there is a lighter side to it all. Forget for a moment the years of depression, forget the waiting for a tramcar in a wet street and the cold ride on the wooden-seated open-top deck. Instead, recall the sunny ride through Gosforth Park or beside the sea at Whitley Bay or Roker. Remember the friendly motorbus threading its way through the colliery villages on its journey to the bright lights of the city. Recollect youthful enchantment in the great cavern of Newcastle Central when it pulsated to big green steam locomotives and sleek red-and-white electric trains. Take an excursion into a little bit of the past and look again at Tyne & Wear's transport of yesterday. It is a nostalgic journey perhaps, but nevertheless instructive in reminding us how the present has grown out of the past.

Acknowledgements

I am especially indebted to those who have written about Tyne & Wear's transport in the past, both in the periodicals recording and commenting on events over the years, and in the numerous books on general and particular aspects of the subject. Most of these sources are listed in the bibliography. I am grateful to John Prigmore and the Librarian of the Lyon Playfair Library of Imperial College for granting me access to the resources of the library. My thanks must also go to the good friends and fellow-enthusiasts who have supplied photographs to enliven the pages that follow: to G. H. F. Atkins, Roy Brook, W. A. Camwell, I. S. Carr, C. Carter, C. R. L. Coles, M. Dunnett and G. S. Hearse; to the Tyne & Wear Passenger Transport Executive and, not least, to the Ian Allan Library.

1 'A Spacious, Populous Place . . .'

Our population is only 300,000, including surrounding areas; we have any amount of cheek, and call ourselves the metropolis of the north.

Alderman J. H. Rodgers, Chairman, Newcastle Corporation Tramways Committee, 1914

'Newcastle is a spacious, extended, infinitely populous place; it is seated upon the River Tyne, which is here a noble, large and deep river, and ships of any reasonable burden may come safely up to the very town'. We look up from our guide book as our East Coast train rumbles over the High Level bridge and threads it way over the crossings into Newcastle Central. The new century is still young as we alight from our Joint Stock coach and look around us at the great curving cavern of the station.

At the long through platforms, trains in crimson or teak brown are headed by big-wheeled bright green engines; the thrill of the well-remembered 'Races to Scotland' still seems to inspire every burst of fast running, and the North Eastern Railway is establishing no little of a speed reputation. Already we have been able to rush from London in less than six hours, and Scotland's capital city is only 2½ hours away. But we have come to see the Tyneside city and its surroundings, so our attention turns to the bays at each end of the station where the numerous local trains come and go; sturdy tanks, as well as 4-4-0 and 2-4-0 tender locomotives, their Westinghouse pumps thudding, haul solid bogie coaches or six-wheelers, the latter already becoming scarcer than on some other companies' trains. The platforms are thronged with businessmen from Prudhoe and Hexham, pitmen from Backworth and Sedghill, shipyard workers bound for Walker or Hebburn, holidaymakers off to Tynemouth or Whitley Bay. And all the while, through the station trundles the unceasing parade of freight trains bound for the Forth goods depot which is almost next door, for the coal and shipbuilding industries are thriving. Later we shall explore the ways of these trains, both passenger and goods, to see how they serve the people and the industries of Tyneside and Wearside.

Unlike some other stations calling themselves 'Central', Newcastle's principal station fully lives up to its name. We pass through the main booking hall and the impressive portico into Neville Street and we can soon experience the heart of the city. 'The town extends for more than two miles along the Tyne', we learn from our guide book, 'creeping up the steep banks, broad, handsome and substantial streets spread out on every hand, with exchanges, markets, newsrooms, and other appliances of civilisation, which rival those of any other town in the Empire.' And prominent now among the 'latest appliances of civilisation' are the electric tramcars; they made their debut in a snowstorm as recently as 1901, but already we can take a car to almost any of the city's suburbs.

If we choose to ride the cars we can go even farther, for between 1902 and 1904 the electric tracks are extending right the way to the coast; we can travel out through the rows of terraced houses of the suburbs, past the busy shipyards and engineering works, the coal staiths loading their fleets of colliers on the river. We realise we are not just seeing Newcastle, Wallsend, North Shields and Tynemouth now; already it is becoming one great 'Tyneside'. By 1902 the NER has plans to electrify its railway along here; faced with the competition of the tramcars and, like other railways at this time, contending with rising costs, in 1904 it inaugurates electric operation on its coastal loop, which in the more distant future will form the basis of a Metro as yet undreamt of but already in a germinal phase. Tramway and electric railway are linking city with suburb, town with town, establishing corridors of communication which will form the arteries of a region in the age of the motorbus and the motorcar.

Railways served Tyneside long before there was any thought that they would carry passengers. Their object was to convey coal from the mines to the river for loading on to ships: as early as the Middle Ages 'sea coal' was heating London's homes. By the end of the 18th century a network of waggonways was transporting coal, and the early decades of the 19th century saw the completion of colliery lines that ranked as substantial undertakings, some of them even being incorporated into the main line system which was by then developing across the country. The Hetton Colliery Railway was opened in 1822, the Stanhope & Tyne to South Shields in 1834, the Brandling Junction to South Shields and Monkwearmouth in 1839. Meanwhile the first major main line in the north of England was completed in 1839 when trains began running between Newcastle and Carlisle. In the same year the important local line from Newcastle to North Shields was brought into use, extended to Tynemouth in 1847.

Above:
On the outskirts of Newcastle; at Low Fell around the turn of the century North Eastern 2-4-0 No 153 of Fletcher's '901' class dating from 1881 heads an East Coast 'Scotsman' of Joint Stock six-wheelers.
Ian Allan Library

Below:
'At length we approach Newcastle, where we cross the High Level bridge, one of the masterpieces of Robert Stephenson. It has been called the King of Railway Structures . . .' – *Great Northern Railway Guide,* 1879.

THE HIGH-LEVEL BRIDGE AT NEWCASTLE.

Left:
As the driver sees it: the impressive signal gantry at the entry to Newcastle Central at the turn of the century.

Below left:
'Newcastle is a spacious, extended, infinitely populous place. It is seated upon the river Tyne which is here a noble, large and deep river, and ships of any reasonable burden may come safely up to the very town.' So wrote Daniel Defoe in 1724. This late 19th century view, with sailing vessels and paddle steamers, is dominated by the High Level bridge, with the swing bridge visible just in front of it.

Above right:
A reminder of the network of colliery railways which developed in Tyne & Wear to pioneer the basic principles of the modern railway system. This Victorian view depicts the Hetton Colliery Railway 'showing how a train of loaded wagons draws a train of empty ones up the inclined plane', according to John Timbs' *Wonderful Inventions.* Rope-worked inclines were a long-lived feature of several important colliery lines.

Right:
A historic spot on Tyneside; a Newcastle–Hexham diesel multiple-unit train approaches Wylam past the house which was the birthplace of George Stephenson. With the coming of diesel traction during the later 1950s on the Newcastle–Hexham–Carlisle line, as on other lines in Tyne & Wear, services were noticeably accelerated. *I. S. Carr*

Below:
Surviving into the new century were the last of Newcastle's horse-drawn tramcars, the first of which had appeared in 1878. Of the single-ended reversible type, this one waits at Gosforth on the lengthy route through the growing city to Scotswood. *C. Carter*

With the opening in 1844 of the Newcastle & Darlington Junction Railway a through route was completed between Tyneside and London; passengers could travel between Gateshead and the metropolis in about 12 hours. Northward they could soon take the Newcastle & Berwick line which was completed in 1847. It was not until 1849 that trains could cross the Tyne with the opening of Stephenson's High Level bridge, while Newcastle Central station was opened in 1850.

The North Eastern Railway was formed in 1854. Not yet enjoying a monopoly, it faced a threat from the north in the shape of the Blyth & Tyne Railway which in 1864 penetrated into the heart of Newcastle with its own terminus at New Bridge Street, to provide a competing service to Tynemouth and Morpeth as well as Benton, Backworth and Blyth. It was not until 10 years later that the company was acquired by the North Eastern. South of the Tyne, the steep Derwent Valley line was opened in 1867, and the line from Monkwearmouth to Southwick and Hylton in 1876, followed by the bridge over the Wear into Sunderland in 1879.

Under the influence of the coal trade and the shipbuilding and engineering industries, Tyneside and Wearside were booming in the latter decades of the 19th century, and by the time we arrive on the scene the area's total population is getting on for one million. Docks spread down the river banks; set up by an Act of 1850, the Tyne Improvement Commission undertook its task vigorously: Northumberland dock was opened in 1857, Albert Edward dock in 1884. In 1859 the NER opened its own facilities at Tyne Dock, which went on to set records as a coal-exporting port: in the early part of our century it was sending out more than seven million tons a year. The NER also built coal staiths at Dunston in 1891, which were further extended in later years. Before World War 1, the Tyne as a whole was exporting more than 13 million tons of coal a year.

Shipyards at Wallsend, Hebburn and Jarrow made their own demands on the railways, not only for transporting thousands of workers, but for conveying heavy and bulky freight; the NER's rolling stock had to include wagons capable of accommodating massive castings and such items as ships propellers, sometimes involving out-of-gauge loads calling for special traffic measures. In the engineering industry, the great works of Armstrong Whitworth were paramount, but Tyneside was also appropriately the home of locomotive builders: the firm of Robert Stephenson & Co was founded as early as 1823 on a site at Forth Street in Newcastle, and when the company found space too cramped and moved to Darlington, the site was taken over by another long-established name, R. W. Hawthorn Leslie & Co, which had been founded in 1817. The NER inherited its Gateshead works from one of its constituents, the York, Newcastle & Berwick Railway, and many renowned engines emerged before production ceased in 1910.

Within the growing towns, horse-drawn tramcars were introduced: Newcastle had its first in 1878, Sunderland in 1879, South Shields in 1883. Steam tramcars appeared in Gateshead and Tynemouth. But it was electric traction that gave the real impetus to the expansion of the tramways, which in the early years of our century spread a network of tracks across the area. In some cases the initiative was municipal, the local authorities, in their new-found civic dignity, adding the new amenity to their streets: Sunderland introduced its municipal electric tramcars in 1900, Newcastle in 1901, South Shields in 1906. In other cases private enterprise provided the electric cars: in Gateshead and Tynemouth in 1901, in North Shields and Wallsend in 1902, in Jarrow in 1906. Although this dichotomy of interest did not always result in harmony, the benefits of cheap and convenient local transport facilities were far-reaching. In the words of Newcastle's manager, 'the tramcar is the poor man's motor.'

2 The View from Central

We cross the River Tyne by the High Level bridge and run into Newcastle Central station at 4.18am. The approach to this city by night is weird in the extreme. Huge works are fully active, and blast furnaces fill the sky with a vivid glare... The station is full of activity. Huge piles of parcels traffic are being loaded into trains, shunting engines are taking a carriage off here and attaching it there...

Meccano Magazine, 1934

Lesser cities may have boasted of more than one main station, including perhaps a 'Central' that barely lived up to its name, but Newcastle was fortunate in possessing *the* 'Central', a station not only well placed from the point of view of rail and passenger access but also a worthy part of the city's architectural heritage. Designed by the noted architect John Dobson in what contemporaries described as 'the Romano-Italian style, with ornamental work of the Doric order', the station took three years to build at the not inconsiderable cost of £90,000. It was formally opened by Queen Victoria on 29 August 1850, at which time there were only six platforms although five signalmen were kept busy controlling almost a hundred trains a day.

'Which is your largest station?', the *Railway Magazine* asked the North Eastern's general manager, George Stegmann Gibb, in a turn-of-the-century interview. 'Newcastle Central', was the reply. 'It covers an area of 39,360 square yards and the aggregate length of the platforms is 3,000 yards. There are seven signal cabins, with 613 levers, and they are manned by 39 men and 24 boys.' As to the traffic, well over three million passengers were booked in the course of a year, and while the average number of trains was about 700 a day, during the July race week as many as 850 trains were run in and out in one day.

To cope with the ever-increasing traffic, substantial expansion had taken place over the years, especially during the early 1890s, so that by the start of the new century the 15 platforms under a roof expanse of 7½ acres had a total area of 15,000sq yd. The original portico still led to the quadrangle faced by the through platforms and flanked by the east and west bays, but it had been augmented by what was in effect a second quadrangle, known as Tynemouth Square from the fact that it gave access to the platforms used by trains on that line.

The stationmaster, ably abetted by 11 assistant stationmasters, had within his purview some 300 ticket collectors, porters and other functionaries, as well as 170 guards, 20 shunters, nearly 100 signalmen and more than 200 booking clerks. Apart from the expected duties connected with the working of the trains, we can get some idea of the miscellaneous traffic then dealt with at a busy station from the 30-odd clerks in the parcels department who were called upon to handle during a typical year almost a million parcels and packages in addition to more than 8,000 horses and 1,500 carriages, over 20,000 bicycles, nearly 9,000 dogs, over 90,000 cans of milk, and getting on for 6,000 tons of fish, fruit and other commodities.

There were still effectively only three through platforms: the main one was No 8, the longest (some 1,100 feet) and the platform principally used by the East Coast expresses, while Nos 9 and 10 formed an island. All the other platforms were of the terminal type, situated in bays to the east and west ends of the station and incorporating docks for horse and carriage traffic.

The nature of the site affected other aspects of traffic working. Lack of space for any adequate accommodation for locomotives or empty stock necessitated a good deal of light mileage to and from such depots as Gateshead, Heaton and Delaval. Again, the proximity of the Forth goods station, which was practically the next-door neighbour to Central, obliged goods trains to and from north, east and south to pass through the precincts of the passenger station, adding their not insubstantial quota to track occupancy within the station limits.

During the first decade of the new century, traffic working at Central was transformed by three major developments. In 1904 electric operation was introduced on the busy Tynemouth line. In 1906 the King Edward bridge across the Tyne was completed, obviating the need for through north-south trains to reverse in Central. Then in 1909 the line from the old New Bridge Street terminus of the former Blyth & Tyne Railway was extended to join the main line at a new junction at Manors to make possible out-and-back working of the Tynemouth electric services.

Reversal of north-south trains in and out of Central was an obvious inconvenience; not only did it add to the complexity of train working in an already crowded locality, but it interposed delay to even the most crack East Coast expresses which were in a perennial state of competition – whether overt or implied – with their West Coast rivals. The answer was the construction of a new bridge, with relevant connections, to enable trains to and from the south to enter or leave the west end of the station without reversal, and even to run right through Central without stopping, a hitherto unprecedented notion. The foundation stone for the new structure was laid in 1902, and on 10 July 1906 King Edward VII declared open the bridge which was to bear the royal name, though regular passenger

Above right:
The handsome portico of Newcastle Central station; horse-drawn cabs and open-ended tramcars adorn this Edwardian scene. *R. Brook*

Right:
Apparently tackling its load with ease, No 910 (built at Gateshead in 1875 and rebuilt in 1886) was one of Fletcher's '901' class 2-4-0s which gave good service on the East Coast main line. Here it hauls a heavy express including bogie coaches as well as six-wheelers. *Ian Allan Library*

At speed on the main line.

Below:
Fletcher 2-4-0 No 926 of the '901' class dating from 1873 and subsequently rebuilt, going strong with an East Coast train of mixed NER stock of both elliptical-roof and clerestory type. No 926 was withdrawn in 1914. *Real Photographs*

services did not use the bridge until the following 1 October.

This first run over the new bridge was made with no great ceremony (the junketings were long over) but a good number of people at Central watched the train depart from the west end of the station. Various company officials boarded the seven-coach mixture of North Eastern and Great Central stock headed by locomotive No 1930, and the way was cleared by no less a personage than the NER's general superintendent, H. A. Watson, who manipulated the levers of the new electro-pneumatic signalling installation to allow the train to set off round the sharp curve on to the bridge. Even then only expresses were routed this way, and it was the start of the New Year before local services were admitted.

Four tracks crossed the four spans and their stone viaduct approaches, while on the Gateshead side a triangular junction gave access to the York main line and the High Level bridge. On the north side of the river the cramped location necessitated laying the new lines through one corner of the warehouse of the Forth goods depot, the foundations being taken right down into the cellars. The odd part of the building thus isolated by this intrusion was put to good use as offices for the depot staff.

The electro-pneumatic signals we have just seen at the hands of the superintendent were part of an extensive scheme carried out in the early years of the century to modernise the complicated signalling which had grown up at Central and its approaches. Of the seven cabins, the main one was No 1 at the east end of the station and this contained 244 levers. No 2 had only 57 levers but controlled the main through platforms, while No 3 was situated at the west end to control the approach to the King Edward bridge. At the east end were No 4 and the High Level cabins, while there were also cabins at Dean Street and Forth Banks.

By 1909 a new No 1 cabin with more than 250 levers was built on a gantry at the east end of the station to replace four of the old ones: Nos 1 and 4, Dean Street and High Level. This incorporated electro-pneumatic operation, which had already been brought into use in boxes 2 and 3. The system was extended to cover not only the whole of Central but also Gateshead and the boxes at Manors. The North Eastern had adopted electro-pneumatic signalling as early as 1905 when it had been installed at Tyne Dock. One of the five boxes so fitted, Pontop Crossing, also had the distinction of controlling power-worked level crossing gates, then the only such installation in Britain.

Supposing on our journey back in time we have taken up our posts as spotters at Newcastle Central one summer in those Edwardian days, what could we have jotted down in our notebooks? Let us start our vigil at midnight, for within a few minutes we can see the arrival at 12.17 of an East Coast express, the 6.50pm from Kings Cross; described as a 'horse, carriage and motorcar train' (the concept of Motorail clearly has a respectable ancestry) and bound for Edinburgh, it is a 'summer only' service and is particularly popular with those gentry travelling north for the start of the grouse shooting on 12 August. About an hour later, at 1.17am comes a sleeping car express, the 7.55 from Kings Cross with through sleepers for Perth, Inverness and Fort William. Then begins almost a 'rush hour' of southbound traffic with three trains in half an hour, all from Edinburgh, all going to London and all with sleeping cars: we see this trio depart at respectively 1.34, 1.44 and 1.54. All three are due at Kings Cross between about 7 and half past. If we can keep from dozing off in the next two or three hours we can witness the arrival of two more East Coast expresses, one at 4.43 and the other at 4.58. Truly, night travel is popular in the holiday season.

But most likely we shall have spent the night hours in the healthy sleep needed by growing youngsters, and have waited until a civilised hour in the morning before beginning our spotting session at Central. From early morning the numerous 'locals' have been bringing in their workaday crowds, and we shall be exploring their lines after we have sated ourselves on the outward glamour of the long-distance expresses. Now at 11am we eagerly await the arrival at 10 minutes past of the morning Scots express; this started as the 5.5am from Kings Cross. Here it takes a well-earned few minutes rest, for it is a real flyer; we are proud to know that it makes a record section of fast running over the 80 miles from York to Newcastle which it covers in only 82 minutes. Now after its brief halt at Central it is off again at 11.17, bound non-stop for Edinburgh, eating up that 125 miles in only 138 minutes.

At midday we see two more flyers, this time southbound. At 12.33 in comes the 'midday Scotsman' from Aberdeen destined for London and complete with mail vans, while very shortly after, the 12.46 gets away for Kings Cross. A short break for lunch now, until at 1.55 another southbound express pulls in, this time the 10.25 from Edinburgh, due to depart from Central at 2.10. An hour later and yet another southbound express from Edinburgh comes in at 3.11, to leave again at 3.17 for London. Very soon after, it is the turn of the northboud direction again with the arrival of the 3.21, the 9.50am from Kings Cross. Now we reach the real highlight of the day when at 3.30pm comes the 'Flying Scotsman', not yet officially named and still prosaically the 10am from Kings Cross, but the most famous of all the East Coast expresses and already with a 50-year reputation behind it. Departure from Central is scheduled for 3.39, when it is away on its non-stop dash to Edinburgh, which it is due to reach at 6.15. At this period the 393-mile journey is down to only 8¼ hours after the 'racing days' which are still fresh in the memory of many. After the 'Scotsman' has departed, perhaps the later trains are something of an anti-climax, but we still have to see the 4.58 from

Above:
An NER flyer in its heyday, No 2103 was one of Worsdell's renowned 'R' class 4-4-0s long evident on the main line through Newcastle. Dating from 1901, No 2103 had 6ft 10in driving wheels. It is here hauling a typical set of clerestory bogie coaches.
Ian Allan Library

Below:
Biggest of the NER 4-4-0s, the 'R1' class is exemplified here by No 1237 of 1908, seen at the head of a heavy train of East Coast Joint Stock.
Ian Allan Library

KENNING TYRE SERVICES
116 DOMINION ROAD, WORTHING, WEST SUSSEX, BN14 8JR
Telephone: Worthing (0903) 31621

VAT Reg. No. 126 2539 35

Name

ORDER No.

Address

VEHICLE REG No.

MAN	PROD	SIZE	CD	UNIT PRICE	UNITS	DESCRIPTION
						Truck Valve Remov

Comments

SALES TOTAL

VAT TOTAL

INVOICE TOTAL

The vehicle wheel nuts have been tigh[tened] setting by use of a torque wrench. Pleas[e] most vehicle manufacturers recommend checked for tightness after the first 5[0]

This has been read and understood.

Received by

Customer's Sig[nature]

Proprietors: Kennings Limited   Registered Office: Gladstone Buil[ding]

KENNING TYRE SERVICES

116 DOMINION ROAD, WORTHING, WEST SUSSEX

Telephone: Worthing (0903) 31621

VAT Reg. No. 129

Name

Address

PRODUCT CODE					DESCRIPTION
MAN	PROD	SIZE	CD		
					Truck Tyre Repairs

Comments

The vehicle wheel nuts have been … use of a … most vehicle manufacturers … checked for tightness …

This has been read and understood.

Received by ……………… Customer's ………

Tyneside motive power at rest.

Above:
The elegant lines of the 'R' class 4-4-0s, with their large brass-beaded splashers and brass safety valve casing, are well brought out in this view of No 2011.
Ian Allan Library

Below:
The NER pioneered the 4-6-0 for express passenger traffic with its 'S' class. Photographed by W. J. Reynolds at Gateshead in 1908, No 2003 dated from 1899. Later in LNER Class B13, it was scrapped in 1931. *Ian Allan Library*

Scotland to London, and we can round off our day with the arrival of the 9.05 up and the 10.48 down.

And what sort of engines have we been noting during our lengthy vigil? We have no Ian Allan ABCs yet, but we do have J. S. MacLean's *Locomotives of the North Eastern Railway,* first published in 1905, to tell us the essential facts about our favourite engines and to recount their exploits, leaving us secure in our belief that there never was such a railway as the North Eastern. Big green 4-4-0s and Atlantics, among the biggest and fastest of their kind, dominate the main line. North Eastern 4-4-0s have seemed to be getting bigger year by year. There were the 20 engines of the 'M1' class, for instance; built between 1892 and 1894, MacLean tells us they were the first express locomotives in England to have a weight in working order (including tender) exceeding 90 tons, and they had played a notable part in the 'race to Aberdeen' in 1895. Products of the NER's Gateshead works during the reign of Wilson Worsdell, they established the type tradition with their long combined splasher over the big coupled wheels, and with the roomy side-window cab which gave locomotive crews on the windy East Coast route welcome protection unsurpassed on some lesser railways where the skimpy cab appeared to be a minor afterthought. Among the exploits of this class we learn from MacLean that No 1625 on 21 July 1903 'accomplished the distance between Edinburgh and Newcastle in 2 hours 12½ minutes with the 8am breakfast car express.'

Then there were the members of the 'Q' class, built in 1896–97, distinguished by the addition of a clerestory to the cab roof and by a brass-capped chimney. No 1871 had regularly maintained a schedule of 43 minutes for the 44 miles between Newcastle and York. Even more striking were the two members of Class Q1, Nos 1869 and 1870 of 1896; these had driving wheels of no less than 7ft 7in diameter, the largest on a coupled engine, and they were 'the only *racing* locomotives that have ever been built by a railway company.' Although the racing days were now over, on a trial run between Newcastle and Tweedmouth No 1869 had averaged almost 70mph, while on a day in 1904 it had run from York to Newcastle on the accelerated Leeds–Edinburgh express in less than 81 minutes, equivalent to 60mph.

Between 1899 and 1901 appeared perhaps the most celebrated of the North Eastern 4-4-0s, the 30 engines of the 'R' class, this time with driving wheel diameter reduced to the still respectable figure of 6ft 10in and with a reversion to the elliptical-roof cab. The first of the class, No 2011, established a mileage record in its first two years of life by running nearly 140,000 miles; setting off from Newcastle it went non-stop to Edinburgh at an average speed of over 50mph, then returned to Newcastle with the 'Scotsman' before going on to Leeds and then back to Newcastle in the same day. MacLean had seen locomotives of this class make up time between Edinburgh and Newcastle with trains of up to 380 tons. Even more massive machines were the 10 designated the 'R1' class locomotives built in 1908; while generally similar to the 'R' class, everything about them seemed to have been scaled up, so that the great boiler dwarfed even that big cab, and the brass-beaded splashers would not have disgraced a paddle steamer. The biggest 4-4-0s of their time, these fine engines represented the peak in this wheel arrangement on the North Eastern, and even overshadowed the 4-6-0s: the NER was the first to introduce the 4-6-0 specially for passenger working, but though engines of this wheel arrangement did good work on East Coast expresses, they enjoyed more renown on fast goods working, such as the fish trains from Tynemouth to the south, for like its partners in the Anglo–Scottish route the North Eastern favoured the Atlantic.

'Engine No 532, the pioneer of the "Atlantic" type on the NER, left the Gateshead shops on Tuesday, 3 November 1903', writes MacLean. Known as the 'Gateshead Infant' because of its impressive size, No 532 was the first of the 'V' class and heralded the start of the NER's Atlantic era on the heaviest trains. No 532's first run on an important East Coast express, MacLean records, was on Thursday, 10 December 1903, when it left Newcastle on the 9.30 to York, returning on the 'Flying Scotsman' at 1.57; this train weighed over 300 tons, but the Atlantic soon showed its powers by gaining six minutes on the booked time. Class V was followed by Classes V1 and Z, and the Atlantics held their foremost place until the advent of the Pacifics during the 1920s, and were still going strong in the 1930s and 1940s.

As to the trains behind these locomotives, the start of the new century witnessed a transformation taking place in the passenger stock used on both the East Coast main line and on the North Eastern's own domestic services. For the 'Scotsman' services, new East Coast Joint Stock trains of vestibuled clerestory-roofed bogie vehicles, including 12-wheeled dining and sleeping cars, took the place of the traditional six-wheelers. The NER also favoured the clerestory for its new stock, and indeed for a railway whose main business was freight, the North Eastern generally did remarkably well by its passengers. True that corridor stock was usually absent on even the longer distance runs, but the clerestory bogie coaches in their deep crimson livery set a standard of comfort that compared well with any other company. Their designer, David Bain, later went to the Midland and carried on his good work there. Earlier NER stock, apart from the six-wheelers which were decreasing in ubiquity faster than on some other railways, included flat-roofed bogie coaches, some with the prominent 'bird cage' look-out at the guard's end, while later practice deserted the clerestory and reverted to a semi-elliptical roof. While therefore our typical train might be made up of a neat rake of four or five clerestory coaches, there was still plenty of variety to be seen.

Above:
'The Gateshead Infant', they dubbed the first of the NER's great Atlantics when it emerged from Gateshead works in 1903, the biggest NER engine then built and the first of a series of 4-4-2s which were to achieve fame on the East Coast route. Sister-engine No 742 of Class V seen here was built in 1904. *Ian Allan Library*

Below:
Originally a Compound dating from 1886, No 1324 was a member of the 'F' class familiar on the main line for many years. No 1324 was photographed in its later days in LNER livery. *Real Photographs*

Variety was also enhanced by the presence of other companies' rolling stock. Although the North Eastern had a virtual monopoly of its territory and the appearance of a 'foreign' engine at Newcastle was ordinarily limited to a North British locomotive exercising that company's running powers over part of the Newcastle–Carlisle line, it was far otherwise with coaching stock. At times indeed, Central presented a veritable rainbow of assorted colours as the wide range of through services brought the coaches of several major companies into its platforms. Brown and white London & North Western stock was used turn and turn about with NER coaches on the joint service between Newcastle and Liverpool, while a similar alternation took place between Great Western and Great Central stock on the 'ports to ports' service from Newcastle to Cardiff and Barry. Red Midland stock ran through to Bristol, and 'salmon pink' London & South Western coaches to Bournemouth. The Lancashire & Yorkshire also employed its coaches on another through service to Manchester and Liverpool.

Choose carefully and we can almost have which colour we want. We can leave Central at 7.30am on the day's first train to Manchester and Liverpool, picking the right day if we wish to travel in an LNWR coach, or we can make a more leisurely start and get the next one, at 10.08, which has the added attraction of that Edwardian amenity the 'Luncheon Car'. Just before this, the 10.05 is a mixture of NER coaches for York and Midland coaches which are taken on via Sheffield, Birmingham, Bristol and Bath to Bournemouth. Alternatively, at 9.30, by making another choice of day we can see either GWR or GCR stock on what the name boards describe as 'Through Train Newcastle, Cardiff, Barry Docks and Bournemouth'. Or at 12.30pm we can settle into the LYR dining car train for the journey to Manchester and Liverpool. As Cecil J. Allen was to write: 'The main line between Newcastle and York in the years preceding World War 1 was the most colourful stretch of track in Great Britain for the variety of coaching stock colours that it saw every day.'

At the time of our late-Edwardian visit to Newcastle Central, some 10,000 holders of season tickets ('contract' tickets) were using the station, an indication of the importance of local traffic. Moreover the number was increasing, in spite of the depredations of the electric tramways which had seduced many short-distance travellers away from the railway. Large numbers of local passengers had been lost from the trains; figures for the total of passengers handled at Central fell from almost four million in 1901 to under three million in 1908. But although about a million passengers had deserted, in fact the financial returns continued to rise, because of the increase in longer-distance traffic, an illustration of the accepted dictum that the railways could not hope to compete with the tramways but should concentrate on developing traffic in areas beyond the scope of the tram tracks. The number of contract tickets issued at Newcastle went up from about 37,000 in 1901 to almost 46,000 in 1908; at the same time the revenue they brought rose from £75,000 to well over £100,000. Hence while the number of tickets was up by nearly 25%, their value increased by 33%.

So how much are we paying for our tickets at this time? For an annual season ticket valid between Newcastle and our home station 20 miles out, we pay £20 first class or £11 third class. To put this into perspective we have to remember that even the third-class rate represented the equivalent of about a month's wages for many people. Nevertheless it was still not proportionately higher than the cost of short distance travel. The weekly workmen's ticket between North Shields and Newcastle Central cost 2s (10p), allowing for the journey there and back each way. For the traveller who chose the electric tramcar, if the daily car ride into the city cost us 2d each way daily, we were paying out almost £5 a year, and that for a journey of perhaps no more than four or five miles. As usual, longer distance travel could be proportionately cheaper, a basic axion among railways attempting to stimulate regular season ticket traffic to and from the more distant homesteads free from the clutches of the electric tramway. Other busy stations at the dawn of the century included Sunderland, which booked nearly a million passengers, and North Shields with almost 900,000.

Those businessmen who found it necessary to travel frequently over a fairly wide area could obtain a first class 'district' ticket which permitted unlimited travel for a year on all lines within a specified district. A Newcastle example enabled us to traverse the lines to South Shields and Sunderland, to Morpeth, and the Blyth and Newbiggin branches, and as far north as Berwick. For this facility we paid £30.

On the lighter side of life, the North Eastern (in common with other railways) helped us select our holiday venue by issuing a wide range of publications extolling the attractions of the various resorts served by its trains. For our own area, for example, we could obtain for a penny each two illustrated booklets under the respective titles of 'The Northumberland Coast and Byways' and 'Tynedale and the Roman Wall', giving us all we needed to know about those districts, including useful information for such specialists as anglers, golfers and cyclists. Indeed the NER showed a particularly soft spot for the cyclist; if we fancied making a cycle tour we could obtain a special ticket enabling us to travel out to one station, and then to pedal to another station to make our homeward journey. 'The need for these tickets was borne in upon me on some of my own cycling runs', the NER's general manager George Gibb revealed. He admitted that the carriage of cycles was something of a problem; railway companies, he believed, 'would give more than thanks to any clever inventor who would produce a feasible plan for carrying many cycles in a small space without damage.' Meanwhile we can take a train from Sunderland (with our bicycle) to Harrogate, enjoy a ride through the Yorkshire dales to Thirsk, from where we get a train back to Sunderland; for this round trip our rail fare is 7s (35p), plus another 2s 6d (12½p) for our bicycle.

The resorts of the Tyne & Wear area attract not only those from our own towns, but also visitors from other parts of the country, and it was naturally in the interests of the railway to develop this traffic. Tynemouth, our turn-of-the-century guide book tells us, 'is much resorted to in summer as a bathing place. To a contemplative mind, few walks can be more pleasing than that among the castle ruins.' And then 'a few miles along the shore are the Marsden Rocks, a grotesque and enormous craggy mass, detached in ages past from the coast by the sheer force of the sea. They are often visited by parties of pleasure.'

Cheap-rate weekend tickets helped to entice the visitor to such delights. The North Eastern had already widely extended the issue of these tickets during the 1890s until by the start of the new century they were available to some 200 stations, including those on the Durham and Northumberland coast and in the Tyne and Wear valleys. Offered at the rate of a single fare for the return journey on all distances of 20 miles or more, the weekend tickets were issued on Friday, Saturday and Sunday and were valid for return on Saturday, Sunday, Monday or Tuesday. 'We took this step with some fear and trembling', general manager George Gibb confessed. But the fears proved to be groundless. 'The fact was that the weekend travelling, stimulated by the cheap fares, also helped to develop more travelling to those stations on ordinary weekdays.'

Below:
Newcastle in the late 1920s: Gresley Pacific No 2563 *William Whitelaw* heads a train from the north over the crossings into Central. The High Level bridge is on the right, while in the background behind the ancient castle is the newly-built Tyne Bridge.
Real Photographs

3 On the Local Lines

For multiplicity of interests, for varied sights, for the perfection of railway management, the district in the basin of the Tyne would be hard to beat.
The Railway Magazine, 1908

Writing their compendious *Express Trains* in 1889, Foxwell and Farrer were not unduly impressed by the North Eastern's main line trains, but they did have a good word for the lesser lines. 'The most creditable North Eastern trains are those which climb up and down the various steep branches', they concluded. 'They soar up successive miles of 1 in 60 with a light-heartedness that would scandalise the decorous companies south of the Thames.' Since that time the express services had been greatly improved, but the local lines had nevertheless retained this reputation for smart working. Even if most of the lines in the Tyne & Wear area did not involve such severe gradients (though there were some, such as the Derwent Valley line, which did) both local and intermediate services produced very creditable performances combined with frequencies aimed at maintaining their patronage. Their importance in the development of the region demands that we turn our eyes away from the East Coast expresses and take a look at the activity in the various terminal platforms at both ends of Newcastle Central.

Tank locomotives of the numerous 'A' and 'O' classes were widely used on the local services, as well as on many longer journeys on which we might have expected to find something larger. But both were thoroughly competent types that were destined to continue their duties long after the North Eastern had ended its separate existence.

Older of the two classes was the 'A' class, consisting of 60 engines built at the Gateshead works to the designs of William Worsdell between 1886 and 1892. 'Double-enders' of the 2-4-2T wheel arrangement, they had 5ft 6in coupled wheels, cylinders 17 or 18in diameter by 24in stroke, a total heating surface of 1,092sq ft, and a weight in working order of 53 tons. After the grouping they became LNER Class F8 and the last of them survived until the late 1930s.

William Worsdell's brother Wilson was responsible for the 'O' class, of which 110 were turned out between 1894 and 1901. Similar in size to the 2-4-2s, they were 0-4-4 tanks with smaller coupled wheels of only 5ft diameter, giving them rapid acceleration which made them popular on stopping trains especially on the more severely graded lines; nevertheless they were capable of a remarkable turn of speed when the occasion allowed. Their cylinders were of 18in diameter and 24in stroke, heating surface amounted to 1,097sq ft, and weight in working order was about a ton more than the 'O' class. They enjoyed an even longer life; after grouping they became LNER Class G5 and nearly all survived in their original haunts well into the days of British Railways. Perhaps their most remarkable exploit was that attributed to No 1837; one day in the mid 1930s, the story goes, one of the great 'A4' Pacifics having failed, No 1837 took over the streamlined 'Coronation' express at Durham and brought it the 14 miles to Newcastle in just 22 minutes, no doubt causing quite a sensation among the waiting spotters!

Members of the 'B' class were also often to be seen working local passenger trains, although they were officially classed as goods engines. Of the 0-6-2T type, they were to be found on such services as those to Blackhill and the corresponding other half of the 'circle' through Consett, a route where no doubt their six small coupled wheels were welcomed on the severe grades. A total of about 60 of the type were built between 1886 and 1890, some at Gateshead and some at Darlington, and some of them had started life as compounds at a time when compounding was being applied to several varieties of North Eastern engines. They were later to become LNER Class N8.

Already veterans by Edwardian days were Fletcher's 'bogie tank passenger engines' (BTP for short), a large class of more than 120 0-4-4 well tanks built between 1874 and 1883. With a weight in working order of 45 tons, they had 5ft coupled wheels, and by the time MacLean was writing they were gradually being converted into 0-6-0 side tanks for a new role as shunters. However, some of them missed this metamorphosis and instead found a new lease of life as the motive power for a series of 'Steam Auto-Cars'.

With a nice feeling for the sporty idiom, the NER gave the appealing name of 'Autocar' to its early examples of what were to become more familiarly and prosaically known as push-and-pull trains. For this purpose the NER coupled an 0-4-4 tank (modified with smaller cylinders for more economical working with its limited load) to a standard clerestory bogie coach suitably adapted by converting the end two compartments into a luggage and driver's compartment complete with control gear; one other compartment was upgraded to first class while the remaining five compartments continued as third class. When traffic required, the train could be strengthened by coupling on another coach. The control gear included regulator, reverse and brake valve, plus a speaking tube to enable the driver to communicate with his fireman. A distinctive appearance was given by the

Top:
Suitably modified in middle age, the distinctive 'BTP' class (Bogie Tank Passenger) 0-4-4 tanks were employed to work the NER's Autocars which provided many local and semi-fast services from 1905 onward. *Ian Allan Library*

Above:
Numerous local services were in the capable hands of the 'A' class 2-4-2 tanks, the first of which had been introduced in 1886 by William Worsdell. This is No 172, built at Gateshead in 1888. *Ian Allan Library*

Below:
The ubiquitous 'O' class 0-4-4 tanks originated in 1894 and numbered over 100 by 1901. Dominating many local and branch services in Tyne & Wear as well as on other parts of the NER, most of them survived well into the days of British Railways as Class G5. Seen in its NER livery, No 2081 dated from 1900. *Ian Allan Library*

pair of circular 'porthole' windows at the driving end of the coach.

The first autocar had been put into local service in the Hartlepools, then in 1905 the new units made their appearance on Tyneside to work the newly-completed branch from Gosforth to Ponteland. In 1906 autocars were announced for the branch service from Tynemouth to Blyth, with a noticeable increase in frequency from only 6 runs a day to a generous 17 trains daily. 'This is the answer', wrote *The Engineer,* 'to recent attempts to get the Tynemouth tramway service extended to Blyth and to establish a service of motor cars between the two places.' The North Eastern may not have been an advocate of competition, but it was clearly not above responding when the need arose.

The elegant little autocars were not confined to purely local duties. The engines had a good turn of speed, and with some two tons of coal in the bunker and almost 1,000 gallons of water in the tank, they possessed a useful range of action. Hence they were let loose on several quite lengthy main line runs, where they were frequently interspersed with the more conventional trains to augment the service. They ran from Newcastle to Sunderland and Durham, while their especial ability to make a quick change of direction was put to advantage in the operation of two unusual through services where intermediate reversal was necessary: they worked between Morpeth and Newbiggin, involving reversal at Bedlington, and between Morpeth and Blyth, with reversal at Newsham.

At the other end of the scale from the small Fletcher tanks on the autocars, the North Eastern also established a tradition for big tank locomotives, a practice which persisted until the final days of steam. Under Worsdell and Raven a succession of big tanks for both passenger and goods work came into action, all sharing a distinct family likeness in their handsome lines with straight frames, massive tanks and spacious-looking cabs. They were solid business-like machines capable of handling any job in sight, whether it be lugging coal down to the Tyne or rushing business men from Newcastle to Middlesbrough.

First came the 4-6-0 tank locomotives of Class W in 1907, with coupled wheels only just over 5ft in diameter for coping with severe gradients; they were later modified to become 4-6-2T with larger bunkers and were taken into the LNER as Class A6. The black-coated 'X' class 4-8-0 tanks originating in 1909 (and later LNER Class T1) had even smaller wheels and were three-cylinder machines intended for heavy shunting duties. The Class Y 4-6-2 (later LNER 'A7') were generally similar in outline and were designed for local freight haulage – they were capable of getting away with trains of up to 1,000 tons.

'A powerful type of passenger tank engine, which is known as Class D, has been designed by Mr Vincent Raven, to work the heaviest local passenger traffic on the NER in place of passenger tender locomotives', reported *The Engineer* in 1913 when describing the first of this new type (complete with the marvellous detailed large-scale drawings which were a feature of that journal and a delight to the railway enthusiast). Of the unusual 4-4-4T wheel arrangement and with three cylinders and 5ft 9in driving wheels, they were elegant machines in their smart green livery lined out in black and white. Indeed Cecil J. Allen described them as 'one of the most handsome tank engine types ever seen on a British railway', a judgment from which no North Eastern supporter would dissent. A total of 45 of them were built up to 1922; the LNER later rebuilt them as 4-6-2 tanks to give them greater adhesion and classified them 'A8', but happily the rebuilding did nothing to spoil their good looks.

During our midnight vigil at Central we could have witnessed the departure of the Irish boat train via the Newcastle-Carlisle route. This leaves at 1.10am for Carlisle, thence to Stranraer for the crossing to Belfast, while a little later at 2.30am we could see the arrival of the return working. If we feel like taking a trip to Ireland ourselves, the first-class return fare Newcastle–Belfast will cost us £2 6s 2d (£2.31). The two boat trains at this time have the distinction of being the fastest on the Newcastle–Carlisle line, and the only ones to do the journey without a stop, covering the 60 miles in 1½ hours. Before they were introduced in the last years of the old century the fastest train had been an express composed of meat vans which had been allowed 98 minutes with one stop.

The best ordinary passenger trains between Newcastle and Carlisle are nevertheless making the journey in 1½ hours with two intermediate stops, generally hauled by an 'R' class or one of the older 4-4-0s, and including modern bogie clerestorys or even the newer elliptical-roof coaches. But as far as Newcastle is concerned, the line also carries a substantial residential traffic to and from stations out to Hexham, 21 miles from the city. Apart from Hexham itself, stations such as Stocksfield, Riding Mill and Corbridge deal with a flourishing commuter trade. The local service to Hexham at this period consists of 16 trains a day each way calling at all intermediate stations and taking about 55 minutes for the journey. In addition a few 'expresses' call only at Blaydon and/or Elswick, and there is even the odd non-stop, all of them taking only about half an hour. The last train of the day to Hexham leaves Central at 11pm. Motive power is provided by the ubiquitous tank locomotives of the 0-4-4T Class O and the 2-4-2T Class A.

Taking a train for Hexham, we depart from the west end of Central, continuing straight on past the junction for the King Edward bridge and the Forth goods depot, and on parallel with the Tyne alongside Armstrong Whitworth's Elswick works which extends for more than two miles to Scotswood. At the small Elswick station with its single island platform, tradition required all up trains to stop for ticket collection before proceeding into Central. At Scotswood Junction

Right:
An autocar in action; a 'BTP' class 0-4-4T propels its clerestory-roofed 'car' while hauling an additional six-wheeler. *Ian Allan Library*

Big tank engines for goods work.

Below:
The Class X three-cylinder 4-8-0 tanks, intended for heavy shunting duties, were the last locomotives to be built at the NER's Gateshead works which closed in 1910. This is No 1352 of 1909. *Real Photographs*

Bottom:
No 1175 was one of the small-wheeled three-cylinder Class Y 4-6-2 tanks designed for hauling heavy mineral trains over the steeply graded lines of County Durham. *Ian Allan Library*

Big tank engines for passenger traffic.

Below:
'One of the most handsome tank engine types ever seen on a British railway', Cecil J. Allen called Raven's 'D' class 4-4-4Ts introduced in 1913. A total of 45 were built up to 1922. This is No 2143 of 1913.
Ian Allan Library

Centre:
To provide greater adhesion, the LNER rebuilt the 'D' class 4-4-4Ts (by then its 'H1' class) to the 4-6-2T wheel arrangement, when they became Class A8.
Ian Allan Library

Bottom:
Though classified as goods engines, the 0-6-2 tanks were to be seen working passenger trains on the more heavily graded lines. No 855 was a member of the 'B' class and dated from 1888. *Ian Allan Library*

Below:
NER 'A' class 2-4-2T No 205 runs bunker-first with a local, including a horsebox, a high elliptical-roofed coach and two clerestory coaches. *Ian Allan Library*

Centre:
Built by Hawthorn Leslie of Newcastle in 1884, No 1495 of MacDonnell's '38' class of 4-4-0s was one of the last batch of express locomotives to be built for the NER by an outside firm. It is seen in service on the Newcastle–Carlisle line, on which engines of this class were regularly employed; the characteristic clerestory bogie coaches were already used on the line by the early years of the century. *Ian Allan Library*

Bottom:
The North British Railway had running powers over the NER between Hexham and Newcastle, bringing the exotically-named 'Scott' class 4-4-0s into Central on through trains. This is No 899 *Jeannie Deans.*
Ian Allan Library

we see the branch to North Wylam, which carries about a dozen passenger trains each way daily, going off on our right as we cross to the south bank of the river, where the Blackhill line curves away sharply to our left.

Again about a dozen trains a day make their way up the Blackhill line, which winds through Swalwell and up the valley of the Derwent. Here indeed Foxwell and Farrer could have seen their light-hearted little trains making short work of their way up long grades. The climb begins almost as soon as the line is over the Tyne and past Swalwell; then for the seven or so miles from Rowlands Gill through Lintz Green, Ebchester and Shotley Bridge to Blackhill, it is an almost continuous climb of 1 in 66. With eight stops, trains from Newcastle are normally allowed 45 minutes for the journey.

But back on our way to Hexham we encounter no such formidable grades as we continue along the south bank of the Tyne. We join the original Derwenthaugh line of the old Newcastle & Carlisle Railway, by now used only for freight, and enter Blaydon station, which a contemporary describes as 'somewhat antiquated'. We continue through Ryton and Wylam, soon after which we join up with the North Wylam branch we left at Scotswood, another reminder of the changing approaches to the city. Then through Prudhoe, Stocksfield, Riding Mill and Corbridge, we round a sharp curve to enter Hexham, which according to our period guidebook is 'a quiet, small country town, with a population of 7,000.' Hexham is the terminus of services on the Allendale branch, as well as connecting with the North British line to Riccarton Junction and the Waverley route, from which the NBR sends its trains on their incursion into England as far as Newcastle. With only two platforms and two bays, Hexham station, our well-informed authority tells us, is 'ludicrously inadequate' for handling its busy traffic.

We have already glanced southward along the Derwent Valley line when looking at the route to Carlisle, and maybe we took the opportunity of travelling on one of the shortest of suburban services, that to Dunston. A passenger station was opened at Dunston as recently as 1909, so we could sample it in all its pristine glory before the potent industrial atmosphere has done its worst. Dunston marks the site of the NER's extensive coal-loading staiths on the Tyne, and the passenger service to the new station is provided by an autocar shuttling to Gateshead and across the river into Central.

By contrast a long-established heavy passenger traffic characterises the line going off southeastwards to South Shields. This serves en route the important localities of Hebburn, Jarrow and Tyne Dock with their busy shipyards and coal berths. Already a half-hourly service obtains on the line, but from the start of 1910 we see this increased to a 20min frequency. In addition to the basic trains there are also of course numerous extras at peak periods. But even before the increased frequency, the intensity of the service is no less worthy of remark. The first train in the morning

Above left:
A vintage view of Wylam station showing the staggered platforms and elevated signal cabin. Pole in hand, the shunter stands ready beside the 'birdcage' brake van. *Ian Allan Library*

Between South Shields and Sunderland.

Above:
'A8' class 4-6-2T (formerly NER Class D 4-4-4T) as BR No 69855 pauses at East Boldon with a train from South Shields to Sunderland in 1958, shortly before replacement by diesel multiple-units. The station clearly maintains the well-kept NER look. The South Shields–Sunderland passenger service was withdrawn in 1965. *I. S. Carr*

Below:
A South Shields–Sunderland push-and-pull train, propelled by 'G5' class 0-4-4T No 67253, stands at Monkwearmouth in 1958. The elegant arch of the footbridge is noteworthy. The station closed in 1967 and was reopened as a museum in 1973.
I. S. Carr

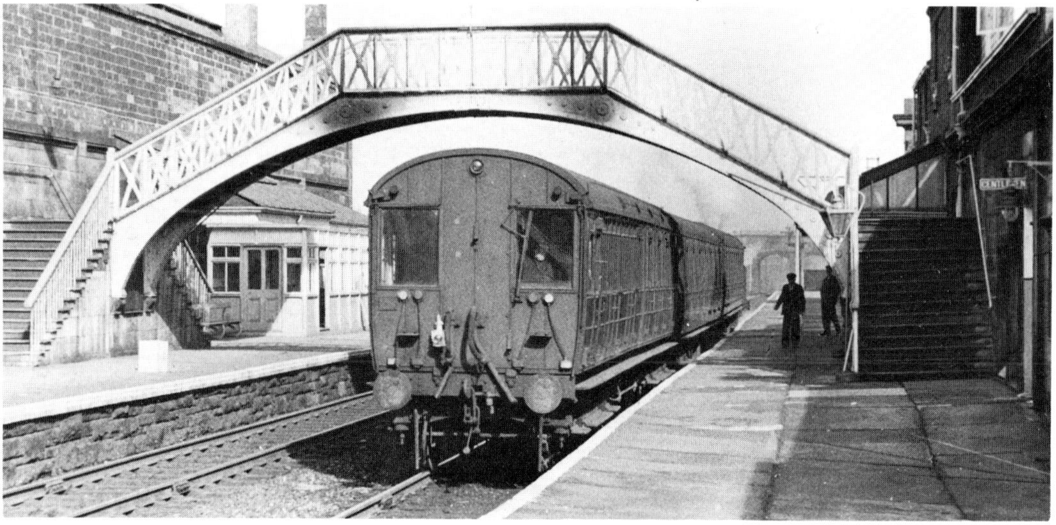

from Newcastle to South Shields departs from Central at 4.55am, while the first arrival comes into Central at 5.21, followed by others at 5.50 and 5.55. The last departure from Central is not until 11.45pm, while the last in from South Shields reaches Central at five minutes after midnight, in summer often well filled with the last evening trippers who have been enjoying the sea breezes on the front at South Shields.

While at South Shields some of our trippers may have made a journey on the South Shields, Marsden & Whitburn Colliery Railway, which not only transported coal but for many years offered a public passenger service to those who wanted a glimpse of the sea. The Whitburn colliery it served happened to be conveniently situated near to Marsden Bay, a locality which (as our old guide book has told us) is 'often visited by parties of pleasure', and on a fine Sunday the line did a lively trade with excursionists. From its terminus at Westoe Lane, where electric locomotives of its owners the Harton Coal Company shuttled coal trains over the connection to the NER in the town, the steam-worked 'main line' ran for about three miles along the coast to Marsden and Whitburn colliery. Saddle tanks and ex-NER 0-6-0s hauled four- and six-wheeled coaches obtained from the NER, the Great Eastern, the North British and the Great North of Scotland.

The Marsden railway will later attain the distinction of being 'nationalised' before the advent of British Railways. Since it was owned by a coal company, it came under the control of the National Coal Board when that body was established at the start of 1947. The passenger service continued until 20 November 1953, although from the 1920s we shall see most of its business being taken over by the paralleling buses along the coast road.

Back at Pelaw our line from Newcastle splits into three: one way goes the way we have seen via Tyne Dock to South Shields, one heads south to Washington and Penshaw, while the middle line goes on via Brockley Whins to connect with the line coming south from South Shields, through East Boldon, to Monkwearmouth and over the Wear into Sunderland. Built, so tradition has it, on the site of a brewery, Sunderland station was opened in 1879 on a rather cramped site between two tunnels and below street level. At the time of our visit it is dealing commendably well with some 120 trains a day in each direction at its three platforms.

Sunderland can also boast an impressive new bridge which, like Newcastle's High Level, is a double-decker, with railway on top and roadway beneath. Completed in the summer of 1909 at a cost of nearly £500,000, and named the Queen Alexandra Bridge to complement Newcastle's King Edward Bridge of the same period, it was a joint venture on the part of the NER and Sunderland Corporation since the scheme involved not only two miles of approach roads but also substantial connecting road works. The main span, with a weight of 2,600 tons, was claimed to be the heaviest of its kind of Britain. Sadly the Queen Alexandra Bridge was to carry no passenger service,

Left:
Another of the long-lived ex-NER 'O' class, 'G5' class 0-4-4T No 67343 prepares to depart from Sunderland's below street-level station with a train for Durham in 1957. *I. S. Carr*

Above:
Among motive power passing to the NER when it acquired the privately-owned Londonderry Railway in 1900 was this distinguished-looking outside-framed 0-6-0 dating from 1859. No 10 with its former owners, it became NER No 2271. *Ian Allan Library*

Below:
Class 'G5' 0-4-4T No 67270 was photographed in 1957 near Penshaw North with a train from Sunderland to Durham; the regular passenger service was withdrawn in 1964. The train has just passed Cox Green Junction where the NCB lines to Penshaw yard and Philadelphia (in foreground) diverged from BR tracks; all lines seen in the photograph have since been lifted. *I. S. Carr*

Above:
At Newsham, the junction for Blyth, BR 'J21' 0-6-0 No 65100 of the type long familiar on coal trains on the former Blyth & Tyne lines heads north with the engineers' saloon in the summer of 1955.
W. A. Camwell

Below:
Edwardian local: NER 'A' class 2-4-2T No 205 spins along with a three-coach train including two clerestory coaches, one an end-door corridor and the other a brake-end with guards' look-out. *Ian Allan Library*

and acted as a relief route for goods traffic only, while even the road portion did not realise its full potential as a major highway.

Southward from Sunderland some 16 trains a day are available to hurry us to Durham, the best of them taking only 25 minutes. As well as the tanks and their clerestory bogie coaches, the autocars also take their part in the service, with the fastest of them making the very creditable time of 26 minutes. To Hartlepool we have a choice of routes, the older going by way of Wellfield while the newer and shorter route along the coast via Seaham was completed as recently as 1903, making a junction with the older line at Ryhope Grange and taking in the formerly separate Londonderry Railway.

Acquired by the North Eastern as from 6 October 1900, the Londonderry Railway worked a seven-mile line between Seaham Harbour and Sunderland, built by the Marquis of Londonderry for the purpose of transporting coal from his collieries for shipment from the docks at Sunderland. The railway also carried passengers, and at the time of the takeover about a dozen trains a day were conveying well over half a million passengers a year. The railway had its own dozen locomotives (many of them of strongly individualistic appearance) and some 20 coaches in addition to its freight stock. The immediate motive for the acquisition was the NER's desire to construct its new coastal line from Seaham to Hartlepool, with the object of opening up further coal measures as well as providing an additional interurban route. Seaham Colliery station was served by coast line trains, while the Londonderry Railway's Seaham Harbour station retained a local service to and from Sunderland worked by the NER.

Sunderland also has the benefit of several of the cross-country services the NER is so liberal in providing. It sits astride the Newcastle–Middlesbrough services, for example, while there are also convenient trains to Harrogate and Leeds. Such services are among those to which the NER applied its 'regular interval' principle, a valuable feature extensively pioneered by this company, although the idea can be traced back to the early days of the Newcastle & North Shields Railway. The Tyneside electric trains with their high frequency of operation (and also their analogy with the competing tramways) were obvious candidates for a regular interval timetable, but within a few years the same principle was applied to many other services. We have already noted it in practice on the Newcastle–South Shields route. In 1912 a regular half-hourly service is running between Newcastle and Hexham, with fast and slow trains alternating. Not only is the principle applied to local runs such as Newsham–Blyth or South Shields–Sunderland, but it is also extended to what a later age will call 'Inter City'. The summer timetable of 1911 shows an hourly fast service between Newcastle and Sunderland and Middlesbrough, with departures from Central at 17 minutes past each hour from 8am until 8pm, the trains being allowed 1½ hours for the 50 miles. They are supplemented by the hourly stopping trains between Newcastle and Sunderland. This rational timetabling is to hold the railway in good stead in meeting the competition of bus operators aware of the business value of keeping things simple for the passenger.

Northward from Newcastle, the Scottish expresses follow (as they still do in the 1980s) the main line through Forest Hall, where they pass under the Gosforth–Benton tracks. Some 15 miles from Newcastle they reach the historic town of Morpeth. In our journeys in Edwardian days we find also a service between Newcastle and Morpeth by a second route that of the old Blyth & Tyne Railway. From the former Bridge Street terminus this line continues through South Gosforth and Benton over the main line, then diverging from our electrified coastal route just after passing Backworth. Thence it turns north through Holywell, Sedghill and Seaton Delaval, to Hartley, where it joins the 'Avenue' branch coming up from the coastal line at Monkseaton. North again we reach Newsham, where the branch to Blyth goes off to the right, and then to Bedlington Junction for the branch to Newbiggin-by-the-Sea. We then turn northwestwards to reach Morpeth.

Two stations were built at Morpeth for the two companies in 1847, one for the York, Newcastle & Berwick Railway and the other for the then independent Blyth & Tyne. After the two companies were absorbed into the North Eastern in 1874, the former Blyth & Tyne station became a goods depot while its companion was enlarged to carry the passenger traffic. By the time of our visit the station is handling well over 150,000 passengers a year, including the residential traffic to Newcastle. And as proof that this is not just an area of collieries, the station is also dealing with an annual load of almost 16,000 cattle and 40,000 sheep.

Some eight trains a day each way we find on this Newcastle–Morpeth route via Backworth, some of them running non-stop over the electrified section from either Central or Manors as far as Benton. The termini of both Blyth and Newbiggin, while generally satisfied with connections from their respective junctions of Newsham and Bedlington on the Morpeth line, also enjoy the occasional through working to and from Newcastle. Here the autocars again come into their own, making two daily 'express' journeys over the 16 miles between Newcastle and Blyth, as well as providing a service from Blyth to Monkseaton to connect with the frequent electric trains to Tynemouth and Newcastle.

On our journeyings we have several times encountered these red and cream electric trains, both in Newcastle and on the lines serving the coast, so we should now turn our attention to this important rapid transit system.

'expresses', some half-dozen a day each way mostly making use of the main line between Heaton and the junction at Benton, to run for example non-stop between Manors and Monkseaton. On such operations the journey from Central to Monkseaton was covered in only 19 minutes, and to Tynemouth in 26 minutes. These expresses ran not only for peak-hour commuters, but also provided a late-night facility with a departure from Central at 10.45pm (and via Wallsend to North Shields at 11.02) for the benefit of residents enjoying an evening at the theatre. By around 1910 the basic quarter-hourly interval prevailed on the main circle with through trains, while rush hours saw a lively succession: be in Central at six in the evening and we can see five electric trains depart within the space of five minutes.

The work of electrification had been carried out with commendable rapidity. Contracts had been placed at the end of 1902 with British Thomson-Houston for the electrical equipment, to be fitted to the new cars which were to be built by the NER at York. So well did the work go ahead that the very first electric train on the North Eastern was able to run its trials on 27 September 1903, appropriately the anniversary of the opening of the Stockton & Darlington Railway in 1825.

The loss of four million passengers in three years was enough to justify the hustle. In the area covered by the electrified lines the NER had seen its passengers decrease from nearly 10 million in 1901 to under six million in 1903. The fall was attributed to the coming of the electric tramways which were rapidly spreading out from Newcastle all the way down the north bank of the Tyne and along the coast. Newcastle Corporation had inaugurated its first electric tramcars in 1901 and the cars were soon running on all its main roads out of the city, including routes which paralleled the railway through Heaton and Walker to Wallsend, to Jesmond and Gosforth, and along the Riverside line through Byker, along Walker Road to the Wallsend boundary.

From Wallsend the story was taken up by the Tyneside Tramways company, which on 4 September 1902 opened its route between Wallsend and North Shields. This also came uncomfortably close to railway stations like Point Pleasant, Willington Quay, Howdon and Percy Main. Though the cars took about half an hour to travel between Wallsend and North Shields, they offered the convenience of a 10min service throughout the day. Nor did the problem end at north Shields, for here the attack was pursued by another company, the Tynemouth & District, which on 18 March 1901 had started to run electric cars along its route through Tynemouth and along the coast, closely paralleling the railway to Cullercoats and Whitley Bay. Inland again, the Tyneside company in 1902 connected Wallsend and Gosforth by a sleeper-track 'tramroad' cutting across country to do the journey in less than half an hour.

Two features of the tramway set-up must nevertheless have been viewed by the NER with not disinterested satisfaction. Not for the first or only time, municipal boundaries interjected a hiatus into the provision of through services; while physical connection existed at Wallsend between the tracks of Newcastle Corporation and those of the Tyneside company, it was not until after a long period of negotiation that cross-boundary running commenced. On 29 August 1904 (just a few weeks after the electric trains had started) through tramway services began between Newcastle and Wallsend and North Shields. The other problem was more intractable: while both the Corporation and the Tyneside company used the standard gauge, the Tynemouth company adopted the narrow 3ft 6in gauge, so that through running on to its tracks was impossible: a through tram service between Newcastle and Tynemouth or Whitley Bay was out of the question. This impediment was not overcome until the motorbus took the place of the tramcar.

The North Eastern was under no illusions about its ability to recapture the deserting millions. Railways had to resign themselves to losing local traffic to the tramways, while at the same time they should learn from the tramways that improved service could bring in more passengers. That was the message clearly given forth by the NER's consultants for the electrification project, Charles Merz and William McLellan. Electrification of tramways, they pointed out, had greatly extended the radius over which they could compete successfully with the railways. 'Where electric tramways exist parallel to a railway line the effect has been to withdraw from the railway all passengers who wish to travel distances of two miles or under, save probably those whose homes and places of business both happen to be immediately adjacent to a railway station.'

Electrification of tramways, said Merz and MacLellan, had often resulted in their carrying 10 times the number of passengers. However, the amount of traffic diverted from the railways amounted to only about 10% of this increase, the other 90% consisting of 'entirely new traffic created by the increased facilities offered'. Here was the lesson for the railways: 'it is reasonable to assume that improved railway facilities will have a similar effect upon suburban and interurban traffic, even though it may be impossible by any improvement to recover from the tramway all or even the greater part of the two-mile passenger traffic.' Under these conditions, therefore, the NER went in for electrification 'not so much with a view to retaining the short-distance passenger as to developing suburban traffic, and for dealing as efficiently as possible with a frequent interurban service over some 40 miles of line.'

But if traffic was to be stimulated, old traditions had to be discarded. To attract more passengers, the traditional long steam train running at infrequent intervals had to give way to a much more frequent

Top:
The spacious layout of Tynemouth station, with its four tracks and wrought iron canopies, is well illustrated in this view; a six-car stopping train of 1937 stock awaits departure for Newcastle.
W. Hubert Foster

Above:
'More like a well-ordered garden than a railway station . . .' The extent of the floral decoration at Tynemouth station may be judged from this turn-of-the-century view.

Above:
Steam at Monkseaton: 'G5' 0-4-4T No 67281 (an ex-NER 'O' class) propels the stock of a push-and-pull train from Newbiggin (via the Avenue branch) into the sidings in 1958. Part of the Avenue branch would have been electrified in connection with the projected electric service to Seaton Sluice. *I. S. Carr*

On the North Tyne loop.

Below:
In its pristine state (destination blinds have not yet been fitted to the indicators) a train of new 1937 stock pauses at West Monkseaton on a trial run. With its wooden platforms and simple station buildings, West Monkseaton was opened early in 1933 to serve new housing development. *Real Photographs*

Bottom:
A sylvan setting for a Newcastle-bound eight-car train of 1937 articulated stock near Whitley Bay.
W. Hubert Foster

service, with the length of the train adjusted to the loading at any particular time of the day. The basic operational difference between steam and electric traction, Merz and MacLellan continued, was that with steam 'it is customary to maintain a more or less infrequent service of heavy trains during the slack hours, and to supplement these by additional trains during the hours of increased demand', while with electric operation 'a frequent service of light trains is maintained throughout the whole day at regular intervals, increased traffic being met by increasing the number of coaches per train . . . As at least 70% of the population have no business hours, will not consult a timetable, and object to waiting, it is clear that the second system must result in encouraging people to travel.' Translating this admirable amalgam of market research and psychology into practice on the Tyneside lines, they noted that the pre-electrification pattern of an approximately hourly service, supplemented by morning and evening peak-hour extras, had been replaced by a practically quarter-hourly service throughout.

It was a long fight back; from the six million passengers carried in 1904, the first year of electric operation, it was 1913 before the number reached the 10 million mark. 'It would be interesting to know', *The Railway Magazine* was asking in 1905, 'whether the directors and officers of the NER are satisfied with the results that have so far attended the electrification.' The half-year's accounts had shown that passenger receipts were up by about £9,000, and while the cost of electric working was almost £23,000 there was a saving of well over £42,000 on locomotive expenses. However *The Railway Magazine* (which at that period was not noticeably enthusiastic about railway electrification) believed that only £14,500 of the saving could be attributed to the running of passenger trains, and that there was in fact a loss of more than £10,000 on working for the half year. It claimed that running expenses per mile for the electric trains were almost 10d whereas steam locomotive running costs were only about 8½d per train mile.

A more optimistic reckoning is given by K. Hoole in his *North Eastern Electrics* (1961). He points to a 'substantial reduction in running costs per train mile' compared with the former steam trains. Motive power costs, he explains, were down more than 50%: from more than 14d per train mile with steam trains to less than 7d with electric. And although total running costs were up by nearly 12% (a much more intensive service was being worked) gross earnings were up by some 17%.

If the essentials to success were a continuous flow of traffic throughout the day and a varied array of users, then the Tyneside electrics must have qualified. Even if the first-class travellers led by the redoubtable Duke of Northumberland (who headed a successful revolt against the NER's attempt to curtail their accommodation) represented no more than a small minority, they were symbolic of the traffic mix. Commuters to suburban homes and coastal villas, workmen to docks and shipyards, holidaymakers and day trippers to the seaside, all combined to keep the trains busy, as well as to provide peak loads varying from morning and evening business rushes, to an exodus to the sea on a fine summer Sunday.

The nature of the district and the business it offered was neatly summed up by a contributor to *The Railway Magazine* in 1905. 'Tyneside is filled with populous suburbs', he wrote, 'those nearest to Newcastle being given up to manufacturing, and those more remote being engaged either in shipping or as residential suburbs. Along the coast from Tynemouth some rapidly increasing towns have sprung up. And behind them, in the hinterland, are several colliery towns.' It was an area which already owed much to the influence of the railways towards the creation of a 'conurbation' (though this term had not yet been coined) but which still possessed that development potential regarded by Merz and MacLellan as basic to the prosperity of an electric railway.

Eastward from Central the electric trains to the coast followed the main East Coast route as far as Heaton, then continued through Walker Gate, Wallsend, North Shields and Tynemouth. At Riverside Junction the Riverside branch diverged to serve Byker and to parallel the Tyne through St Peter's, St Anthony's and Walker. Something of a poor relation as far as electric passenger services were concerned, with generally a basic hourly service, the Riverside line nevertheless carried a useful workmen's traffic when the shipyards and engineering works were thriving, though it remained primarily a freight line with steam goods trains catering for the essentials of industry.

The busiest and most impressive station on the coastal section was Tynemouth, 'without doubt the prettiest station of any large town in this country', according to an observer in 1900. He was struck by 'its charming beds of flowers, its hanging pendants of floral beauty covering its roof, and hanging all over its supporting pillars.' Another traveller, seeing the station at its verdant best in summer, thought it looked 'more like a well-ordered garden than a railway station.' The North Eastern had an established tradition of awarding prizes for the best-kept and most attractive stations on its system, and before the first decade of the century was out, Tynemouth could boast no fewer than seven first prizes, two second prizes and three special prizes. With its curving platforms and fine wrought iron canopies, the station was opened with the completion of the new coastal line in 1882, when the old station it replaced became the goods depot.

The next station, Cullercoats, achieved a minor taste of celebrity when it was flooded following heavy rain in the autumn of 1900. The station lay in a hollow and the water rushed in to rise above the level of the platforms. A train tried to plough its way through the

Luggage, fish and workmen: all were catered for on the Tyneside electrics.

Above:
Motor parcels van No 23795, built in 1921, is seen in LNER red and white livery. The sliding doors to the compartments are apparent, while the car was fitted with standard buffers and couplings for attachment to ordinary stock such as fish vans.
Crown Copyright, National Railway Museum, York

Below:
Motor parcels van No 2424 of the 1937 pattern was similarly fitted and was intended as a replacement for an earlier vehicle.
Crown Copyright, National Railway Museum, York

Above right:
Motor luggage van 3525 of 1908 coupled to a train of 10 six-wheel compartment coaches for workmen's service. The destination indicator shows 'Riverside', a line on which workmen's traffic was especially marked.
Crown Copyright, National Railway Museum, York

Right:
The more modern version of the 'control set', with four-motor power car No 24273 coupled to a train of ex-NER bogie coaches in red and white livery, photographed in Gosforth depot in 1947.
G. S. Hearse

RIVERSIDE
RAILWAY
LUGGAGE VAN

water, but apparently became derailed just outside the platform. The stranded passengers had to be rescued by means of boats brought up from the nearby beach. Writing in his *Railways for All* some years later, J. F. Gairns recalled visiting the inundated station at this time and found the boatmen 'plying for hire' between train and station, charging '3d per trip' to ferry marooned passengers to dry land.

A new Whitley Bay station was opened in 1910; the old structure, though only dating from 1882, was demolished and its site became the approach to the new station, involving some realignment of the tracks. At Monkseaton, connection was made with steam trains on the 'Avenue' branch for Blyth and Newbiggin. Inland from Monkseaton, where another new station was opened in 1915, the northern section as it left the coastal district became less heavily loaded as it traversed a region of colliery villages; from Monkseaton to Backworth there was a run of nearly three miles with no intermediate station before West Monkseaton was opened in 1933 to meet the needs of new housing development. Then from Backworth to Benton was another two miles without an intermediate station, except for the short-lived Benton Square which lasted only from 1909 to 1915. Another latecomer was Longbenton, which was not opened until 1947. Changes on this section of the route reflected the changing nature of the area, with its development from scattered colliery villages to more modern suburbia. Through Gosforth and Jesmond the line curved southward through the suburbs of Newcastle into Manors and Central again.

The trains themselves displayed a marked degree of individuality that increased their appeal to the enthusiast if not to the maintenance staff. Even the initial fleet showed differences between individual vehicles, and subsequent modifications were quickly made in such details as the arrangement of seating and the substitution of swing doors for the original entrance gates. The needs of increasing traffic called for additional cars in 1909, and more again in 1915 under the burden of heavy wartime loads. Many of the early vehicles were destined for a long life, so that they eventually acquired a distinguished 'period' appeal. Others less fortunate had their career cut short by a depot fire in 1918 and were replaced by new cars to add further variety to the fleet.

The 35 new cars built between 1920 and 1922 to replace vehicles lost in the depot fire took the same numbers as their predecessors but were immediately distinctive in appearance. Not only did they have elliptical roofs instead of clerestories, but they were painted all over in the NER's standard crimson instead of the earlier red and cream. They seemed to encompass the whole gamut of variations; some were motors, either all-third class or composite, and some had a driving compartment at both ends and some at one end only, and some vehicles were trailers.

Built by the NER at its York workshops, the newcomers again had British Thomson-Houston equipment but were more modern electrically; the new control equipment, which was also installed to convert earlier stock, was designed for use with hand notching controllers with series-parallel operation, instead of the semi-automatic control of the older cars. Motor bogies were fitted with ice scrapers and sand boxes to help them through wintry conditions. Internally, reversible seats in the composite cars were upholstered in blue cloth, while in the thirds the seats were rattan covered. An ingenious feature in the composites was the 'convertible' compartment which could be adapted for first class or third according to the demands of traffic; reversible indicator boards showed 'First' or 'Third' as required, and were locked into the appropriate position to prevent any class-conscious practical joker attempting to cause confusion. Seats in the convertible compartment were upholstered in green buffalo hide. Fittings in the cars included brass electroliers 'of a pleasing design'.

Motor luggage vans added their quota of variety to the rolling stock. Instead of passenger accommodation these vans had large compartments for parcels and boxes of fish, and were so fitted that they could also haul ordinary vehicles such as milk vans or fish wagons. Another of their duties was to work a train of ordinary non-electric coaches, at first a string of six-wheelers and later a set of bogie coaches. This unusual entourage was generally only pressed into service for workmen's traffic. Another, and probably unique, variant among the rolling stock could have proved a trap for the unwary passenger, who could enter a car only to find himself enmeshed in a jam of perambulators. The 'pram vans' had reduced seating capacity to allow room for the wheeled vehicles, and were run on certain trains to enable mothers to transport their infants in comfort to the seaside or on a shopping expedition, an amenity on which the railway scored over the rival motorbus.

With the undoubted success of the Tyneside electric system it might have been expected that other lines would be brought within its scope. Indeed, at least as early as 1909 there were rumours that the NER had decided to go ahead with the electrification of the lines from Newcastle to South Shields and from Newcastle to Sunderland, and rumour had it that workmen were already busy reballasting the tracks at Gateshead in preparation for the new trains, while travellers to Sunderland noted that railway officials were counting their numbers. But the NER stepped in to squash the story; yes, it admitted, the question of electrifying the south Tyneside lines had been under consideration ever since the north side lines had been electrified, but so far no decision had yet been reached one way or the other. South Shields, already by 1910 enjoying a 20min frequency on the Newcastle service, was eventually to get its electrics, but meanwhile two other planned extensions to the system had failed to materialise.

The Ponteland branch was a line that never quite made it. In 1902 the NER contracted for the construction of a 'light railway' from Gosforth to Ponteland, and the seven-mile branch was opened for passenger traffic on 1 June 1905, goods traffic having started the previous 1 March. The intention was that the branch should be electrified when the traffic arising from the nearby collieries and housing development became sufficient to justify this step, and a map published in 1904 rather optimistically shows the line as already part of the electrically operated system, complete with sub-station at Kenton and with intermediate stations at Coxlodge, Fawdon, Kenton, Woolsington and Callerton. In the event, a steam autocar was put on to provide a service of some 10 trains daily between Ponteland and South Gosforth, connecting with the electric trains to Central.

In 1913 the line was extended about a mile to Darras Hall, the new section being so laid as to necessitate reversal at Ponteland. Built mostly on embankment, the extension (the Little Callerton Railway) was set out with sufficient space for doubling when traffic increased sufficiently, as it was expected to do in the growing residential area of the Darras Hall estate. For a few years another line continued from Darras Hall; in 1921 the Wallridge mineral railway was opened for some seven miles to serve Kirkheaton colliery, but the line was used for coal traffic only.

By the early 1920s the Ponteland district was already being served by Newcastle Corporation buses, and although in the later years of the decade a Sentinel steam car was providing a through service to Central, traffic on the railway did not justify its continuance let alone any thought of electrification, and passenger train services were withdrawn from 17 June 1929. Ironically, by the 1970s, rapid transit plans proposed using part of the Ponteland branch to bring trains to serve new housing estates at Fawdon and Kenton Grange, with possible extension to Woolsington airport.

Meanwhile, the opposite side of the electric loop had witnessed another might-have-been. In order to assist in the development of the northward part of the coast as a residential area, the NER had proposed a new branch line to serve Seaton Sluice, once a flourishing port but now a growing resort. The branch would have been electrically worked from the start; it would have taken off from the main Tyne loop near Monkseaton, utilising part of the Avenue branch, about half a mile of which would have been doubled before the new line diverged towards the coast for about two miles to Seaton Sluice, with intermediate stations at Briardene and Holywell Bay. With a frequent electric service it was envisaged that the area would have generated a useful residential and pleasure traffic.

Work on the project, which also included the rebuilding of Monkseaton station, was put in hand in 1913. The new branch line was nearing completion when war broke out in 1914, and under wartime conditions and coastal restrictions it was never finished. Monkseaton got its new station in 1915, but Seaton Sluice never got its trains, although landmarks such as unused platforms and a signal cabin remained for many years as a reminder of this ghost railway.

The North Eastern was nevertheless active in other electrification schemes, one of which would have transformed the scene at Newcastle Central and the working of the East Coast expresses. In 1915 electric operation was inaugurated on the Shildon–Newport line, although for freight only; much more ambitious was the scheme which was in the planning stage in the final days of the independent NER for the electrification of the main line between Newcastle and York, using the overhead wire system. This 'electric railway that never was', as R. A. S. Hennessey calls it in his monograph of that title, got lost after the grouping of 1923, and the only tangible reminder of what we might have seen in Central on the East Coast trains was the great electric locomotive No 13. This was destined never to take over its intended duties, and the only time No 13 ever got to Newcastle was when it was brought to Gosforth car sheds in 1947, only to be taken away for scrapping three years later.

5 'The Poor Man's Motor'

I have seen a passenger deposit a large washing-tub and travel with it a mile and three-quarters, man and tub, for one penny. The conductor suggested he would probably bring the wringing machine next trip.
Councillor Richard Mayne, Vice-Chairman, Newcastle Corporation Tramways Committee, 1914

'After many months of reconstruction, and no tramway service at all, Newcastle-on-Tyne inaugurated the first sections of its electric tramways on Monday, 16 December'. So reported *The Light Railway & Tramway Journal* at the end of 1901. A procession of seven cars graced the opening ceremony, with the Mayoress driving the leading car, a feat of some discomfort since the occasion took place under what our observer describes as 'unfavourable weather conditions'; the cars had to plough their way through several inches of snow and slush, and snow continued to fall around them as they traversed the new tracks. The routes radiated from the city centre, mainly to the northern and eastern suburbs, up the Great North Road to the villas of select Gosforth, into densely-populated Osborne Road and Jesmond, and round through City Road and Raby Street in Byker to Heaton. In spite of the wintry conditions the cars acquitted themselves well, and many folk were thankful to take a ride in the new marvel of rapid transit. Once under way the system flourished as further routes were added, and before the end of the decade nearly 200 cars were carrying more than 45 million passengers in the course of a year.

Corporation cars extended to Wallsend, where the story was taken up by private enterprise. The Tyneside Tramways & Tramroads Co began running electric cars in 1902 as we have seen, and had tracks through to North Shields, where they met those of the Tynemouth & District Electric Traction Co, which in turn continued on through Tynemouth to Whitley Bay. The Tynemouth company had started electric operation in 1901. As a result, from Newcastle's Central station there were electric tramways for a distance of some 12 miles to the end of the line on the coast at Whitley Bay.

South of Newcastle, the Gateshead & District Tramways Co had begun electric operation on 8 May 1901; within a few years it was carrying more than 12 million passengers a year on its suburban routes to Saltwell Park and Bensham, along the Great North Road to Low Fell, up to the heights of Wrekenton, and along the main Sunderland road to Heworth. Further down the river, the Jarrow & District Electric Tramways Co started its cars on 29 November 1906 to traverse the town to reach Tyne Dock, where they met their municipal neighbours from South Shields where the Corporation on the previous 30 March had inaugurated its first electric lines. Within half a dozen years the South Shields fleet of 35 was conveying more than seven million passengers annually.

Sunderland Corporation was the third member of the area's municipal trio but the first to start electric tramway operation (as early as 15 August 1900); within 10 years its 70 cars were carrying nearly 15 million passengers a year on its routes through the town and to the sea at Roker. At the southern extremity at Grangetown, municipal tracks met those of another company, the Sunderland District Tramways, which from 10 June 1905 began to work its far-flung little traction empire through Ryhope into the mining area through Silksworth, Herrington, Philadelphia, Houghton-le-Spring and Hetton-le-Hole.

Substantial sums had been invested in the new mode of travel: well over £1 million in Newcastle, more than £300,000 in Sunderland. But the results looked to be justifying the expense; in Newcastle, for example, total receipts per car mile at just over 11d comfortably exceeded operating expenses of 8d a mile. The Gateshead company was presenting its shareholders with a divident of around 7%. As to fares, we could ride 1½ miles or more for a penny; the Gateshead company offered a flat fare of one penny for any distance.

What were the effects of the electric tramways? And were they giving good value for money? Councillor Richard Mayne, when vice-chairman of Newcastle Tramways Committee in 1914, was in no doubt that his municipal cars had greatly improved the city. 'The installation of the system rejuvenated its venerable face, opened out its arteries, cleared away wrinkles, made smooth the rough places, added vigour to its business and pleasure to its social amenities.' The guiding policy in the construction of the system, he said, had been to give ready access to the cars, and as a result few residents were not within five minutes of a tramway. 'Parallel lines extend from the Central railway station in every direction, so that to walk across from one line to another rarely takes five minutes'. Although this policy had involved greater capital expenditure, he believed it was well justified by the benefits to residents, who in turn showed their approval by their intensive usage of the services: on average, every member of the city's population made more than 200 journeys in the course of a year. Not all the routes were profitable in the strict cash sense and some had to be subsidised; although this was to the detriment of the overall account, it was 'to the advantage of the ratepayers in the particular district, and

On Tyneside's tramways.

Above:
Gateshead High Street around 1930 after the opening of the new Tyne Bridge; a Gateshead & District car heads down towards the river to cross into Newcastle, while coming under the railway bridge are two Newcastle Corporation cars on through services to Gateshead termini. The heavy motor traffic of this major thoroughfare is already becoming evident. *R. Brook*

Below:
Still almost a village street look about the Wrekenton terminus, to judge from this photograph taken shortly after the line had been completed. Ready to return to town is Gateshead & District No 36, one of the 1901 cars from the Electric Railway & Tramway Carriage Works. *C. Carter*

Above:
A South Shields car of the World War 1 period; one of four built in 1914 by Brush on Peckham P22 trucks, it had transverse seating on lower deck as well as upper for a total of 60 passengers.

By tramcar to seaside.

Right:
On Sunderland's coastal tramway, a bleak day at Roker in the early years of the electric cars; open-top No 45 reverses to return to town. *R. Brook*

Below right:
In later days central-entrance streamliner No 53 traverses the exposed coast road on its way to Seaburn. *R. Brook*

doubtless to the eventual cash profit of the city.'

Workmen's traffic was an important part of the business, and workmen's fares were a subject on which Councillor Mayne held strong views. In the morning peak as many as a hundred special cars were run for workmen, at fares amounting to ½d for 1¾ miles, 1d for up to four miles, and 1½d for as far as six miles. These fares were available on any car starting its journey before 7am and on any 'Workmen's Car' in the evening. In addition to ordinary tickets, books of coupons were valid for travel on any car up to 8am and on any car between 4.30pm and 7.15pm, as well as between 12 noon and 2pm to enable the user to travel home to dinner.

The provision of these facilities was a substantial burden on the department. 'Out great factories lie near the river at the extreme eastern and western boundaries of the city, and at 5 o'clock at night, just when so many wage-earners other than the artisan or legal "workman" are wanting to be carried, we lift 12,000 at the special fares.' Although this meant crowded – and even overcrowded – cars, it was only by such crowding that it was possible to carry the load at such low fares. Average earnings per car mile on the workmen's cars were sufficient to cover their average costs, but this would not have been the case if the full overhead costs needed to meet the peak load had been charged to them. Under such conditions it was not surprising if the observer was impressed by the preponderance of big double-deckers, with even the open-top decks filled to capacity.

But was this discrimination in fares too restrictive? Low fares for workmen were a boon for those who were able to take advantage of them, but Councillor Mayne argued that there were many other people who were equally entitled to the concession. Many wage earners on low pay – such as clerks, shop assistants, warehousemen and women – were obliged to pay full fare, while many who were more highly paid (earning up to £4 or £5 a week) travelled at very low fares. However, it was financially impossible to extend cheap fares, since this would have involved substantial capital expenditure on new generating equipment and new cars which would result in an overall loss to the system. 'Had greater foresight been shown when workmen's special fares were instituted, it would have appeared more just to have kept them a little higher and to have extended a modified advantage to many wage earners with small wages', said Mayne. What was needed was a 'levelling up'; this may not have been too popular with those who enjoyed the cheapest fares, but the justice of such a move was obvious.

Should a municipally-owned tramway operate at a profit? When managers assembled in conference, or when 'Disgusted' wrote to his local newspaper to complain about high fares or the poor quality of service, we could be fairly sure this question would be hovering in the air. The discussion went to the heart of the philosophy behind municipal enterprise. Among those who held their own views on this topic was Councillor Mayne. 'Whilst the undertaking of a tramways service by the municipality puts upon the council first and foremost the onus of public service, yet every development should be such as will yield to its shareholders (the ratepayers) a profit on their investment.' Any expenditure must therefore aim at obtaining the most profitable return. Although such profits may be in money terms, 'it would be equally "making a profit" if otherwise inaccessible districts were opened out and house-building encouraged in areas less congested than in the city's oldest streets. The profits would then be obtained in a greater rateable value and in healthier conditions.'

If the municipal undertaking showed a profit, said Mayne, there were some people who urged that this profit should be divided among the users (that is, the passengers) in the form of lower fares or longer rides for the money, rather than handed over for the relief of the rates. 'I find it difficult to view the matter from their point'. A substantial sum of money had been invested in the undertaking, and if it had failed, the ratepayers would have been called upon to make good the loss. 'The natural corollary is that if the system had become a profit-bearing concern, these profits are the property of the ratepayers.'

On this basis, the financial soundness of the undertaking was the chief object of his Tramways Committee. The first call on any surplus was the reserve and renewals fund; this had been built up to the healthy figure of £100,000 and the current policy was to maintain it at this level. Only after this aim had been met was any payment made towards the relief of rates. In 1913, for example, £21,000 was put into the renewals fund while £12,000 was paid over to the city fund.

This same point was also elaborated by the committee's chairman, Alderman J. H. Rodgers. He pointed out that the reserve fund was regarded as being for track renewals only, and any other renewals or the rebuilding of cars were looked upon as charges upon revenue. The maximum expenditure on renewals in any one year was estimated at about £25,000, so that four years renewals were kept in hand; what was spent each year was made up again to keep the fund at £100,000. This was a first charge on profits. The retention of the reserve fund, he admitted, 'was a point we had to fight very hard for . . . I know that in some towns the reserve fund has been commandeered from the Tramways Committee, but here our Council accepted the principle that the Committee should keep that £100,000 as the backbone of the undertaking.'

Twenty years later the situation looks rather different, and again this basic conflict inherent in municipal undertakings came to the fore. In 1934 Newcastle City Council voted to take almost £10,000 from the Transport Department's renewals fund in order to avoid an increase in the city's general rate. In view of the prevailing depressed state of the shipbuilding industry in the area, the desirability of avoiding a rate rise was obvious; moreover, as one councillor argued, 'in times of financial stringency why should we not borrow cash from the cash-box of the transport undertaking rather than take it from the struggling ratepayer?' At this time the Transport Department's reserve fund stood at around £40,000, a sadly low level compared with the accepted £100,000 of prewar years. And, as the Transport Manager stated in his annual report, the department would soon be facing hefty calls upon this fund; more than £40,000 would have to be spent on track renewals if the tramways were to be kept going, while if a changeover was to be made to trolleybuses, then the necessary expenditure would be well over £70,000. Any amount spent in excess of the reserve fund would have to be met by borrowing, at further cost to the undertaking in interest charges.

'Newcastle, like other places in prosperous times, has made a milch cow of its transport', commented *Transport World'.* It pointed out that in total a sum of nearly £250,000 had already been paid over by the Transport Department to the Council in relief of rates, quite apart from the expenditure on road maintenance, while well over £400,000 had been paid in rates over the years. Mayne (now an Alderman and still chairman of the Transport Committee) had long before argued that the ratepayers, who were in the position of shareholders, should benefit from profits; but he was still equally adamant that provision for renewals must have first call on any surplus, for only if this principle were adhered to could the undertaking look forward to a healthy future.

'I am a great believer in corporations owning and working their own tramways', Newcastle's Tramways Committee's chairman Councillor (later Alderman) Rodgers had declared in 1911, 'but I also believe that when this is done, it ought to be done on purely business lines.' This, he lamented, it was practically impossible to do; there were demands for profits to be put to the relief of rates or towards providing cheaper services. But, he continued, the ratepayers had the right to expect a return on their investment; they had backed the bills and they were in effect the owners, while the committee were the trustees on their behalf. 'It is our duty as such to see that the best is made of their estate; to so manage them that they will pay their way, and when once placed on a sound foundation, any surplus that there is ought to be handed over to the ratepayers as owners.'

Examining the basis of municipal tramway undertakings in this context, he concluded that many were following a financially unsound policy. Happily these did not include those in Tyne & Wear; his figures for Newcastle were reassuring, and his list of 30 undertakings which he considered were 'doing well' included not only Newcastle but also South Shields and Sunderland. To provide adequately for maintenance and renewal, he contended that an undertaking should earn a sufficient surplus to enable it to put into its reserve funds each year the sum of £200 for each mile of track. On this basis, Newcastle needed a surplus of almost £11,000, South Shields just over £2,000 and Sunderland £4,000. Both the smaller systems were comfortably meeting this criterion, and Newcastle showed a happy su[illegible] of almost £24,000. Moreover, Newcastle's total reserve and renewal fund amounted to the satisfactory figure of nearly £100,000; South Shields had nearly £10,000 in reserve and Sunderland more than £25,000, so they too were firmly based. The Tyne & Wear trio were therefore living up to Rodgers' prime dictum that 'the first consideration of a tramways committee ought to be to make their undertaking financially sound, by the building up of a sufficient reserve and renewal fund.'

Of three other considerations which featured in Councillor Rodgers' philosophy of municipal tramways, one served to give support for those who sought to take profits to relieve the rates. He believed that 'the ratepayers who backed their bills and over whose streets they ran their cars should have some return in the shape of contribution towards the rates.' But this was to follow only after the other three considerations had been complied with, the most important of these three being (as we have just seen) a sound financial basis.

So what were the other two considerations that were engaging the thoughts of his committee? Again both of these were highly relevant to that concept of service implicit in municipal ownership. One was: 'to see that the travelling public is supplied with proper accommodation and facilities'. As instance of their earnest in this direction he recalled the generous cheap fare facilities already on offer. Though representations had been made for the extension of cheap fares, in Councillor Rodgers' view further concessions would have had a disastrous effect on the financial stability of the undertaking. He reiterated his faith in the commercial approach. 'I believe in giving every facility possible to the public, consistent with the yield of an adequate profit; but I do not see why we should run cars at a loss, or even at a loss of profit . . .'

The remaining consideration should be 'to see that good conditions of labour are given to all their workers.' In addition to reasonable hours of work, he believed 'we ought to give them a somewhat higher wage than that paid in the respective districts to men doing the kind of work from which our employees are generally drawn.' He submitted that 'we have no right to raise those men to a position equal with skilled mechanics, who have had several years to serve to learn their trade'. The tramway employee enjoyed regular and secure work, free uniform and paid holidays; 'if we compare the average income of the two, it will be found that the wages and emoluments of the tram employees, who are generally drawn from unskilled labour, will equal the net income of the skilled artisan.' To place him higher, by higher wages or shorter hours, would be 'not only an injustice to the trained mechanics, but quite unfair to the undertakings we have to manage and direct.'

In the light of this comment, let us see how much Newcastle tramwaymen were paid at this time. The starting wage for a motorman or conductor (and Newcastle Corporation employed about 600) was 26s per week (£1.30). This was increased by 1s (5p) every six months until it reached the maximum of 31s (£1.55). Cleaners started at 22s (£1.10), rising to 26s (£1.30). For comparison, it is instructive to see what their opposite numbers on the railways were being paid at the same time. Elite among the railwaymen were of course the engine drivers who handled both the 'Scotsman' and the no less important 'local'; the average rate of weekly wage for the driver was just over £2, although bonus payments could bring this up to around 45s (£2.25). By contrast his fireman got about 24s or 25s (£1.20 or £1.25). Guards were paid around 28s (£1.40) a week, and porters and permanent-way labourers about £1. In the North Eastern's engine and carriage shops at Gateshead, labourers earned also around £1 a week, while mechanics and skilled labourers received up to about 32s (£1.60). By these standards therefore the tramwaymen's pay seemed to be not far removed from Councillor Rodgers' criterion.

These figures incidentally serve to highlight the significance of cheap fares; the £1-a-week labourer, taking his penny daily rides to and from his work, was having to spend no less than one-twentieth of his total income on fares. It was little wonder that the Tramways Committee should feel a duty to provide the best value for money.

Below:
Many local transport routes served the numerous mining villages interspersed with open country, later 'infilled' by newer housing. Parts of Gateshead & District's Wrekenton route retained almost a rural appearance until the final days of the tramcars. Here two of the enclosed double-deckers pass at a loop.
R. Brook

6 Carrying the Crowds

The industrial undertakings in the town itself, and both up and down the River Tyne, are numerous and most important, giving employment to multitudes of men, so that the tramway services constitute an essential feature in the life of the community.
Tramway & Railway World, 1914

During World War 1, when wagonloads of munitions filled the new coal sidings at Dunston, and a naval seaplane base occupied the foreshore at South Shields, local transit systems had to bear exceptional extra loads of workers to and from factories and shipyards which were going flat out to meet wartime demands. In 1914 Newcastle tramways carried nearly 60 million passengers; in 1918, after four years of war, the number had increased to almost 80 million. Yet over this same period the number of cars in service remained practically unchanged. How this vastly increased load was handled makes an interesting study in the development of a street tramway network into a mass-movement rapid transit system, employing such means as maximum-capacity vehicles and two-car trains.

Much of the undertaking's success in tackling the problem was due to the human element; many of the operating staff were called for military service and their places had to be taken by some 300 women conductors, as well as by auxiliary motormen who were often business or professional men, and who, as Tramways Committee chairman Councillor Mayne put it, 'did a very useful bit, by rising in the mornings at 4.30 and taking out workmen's cars'. To cater for the needs of munitions workers, the early morning peak service was greatly increased; instead of the prewar 95 early morning cars, every available vehicle was put on to the road, so that the average number rose to more than 170. Even so, there was still overcrowding; given the shortage of staff and the impossibility of introducing new rolling stock, this was inevitable, but measures had to be taken to ensure that peak loads could be handled as expeditiously as possible.

The problem was confounded by the fact that the major factories served were concentrated along the riverside, so that the great bulk of the traffic had to be carried on the one main route running parallel to the Tyne. Thus the Scotswood Road, past the extensive Armstrong-Whitworth works at Elswick, groaned under a constant succession of peak-hour cars. Further congestion threatened at Central station, where apart from interchange with rail services, most of this traffic converged to join other routes.

Towards the end of 1915 one of the answers to the overloading problem appeared in the form of a pair of coupled cars, a sort of primitive ancestor of today's Metrocars, and a distinctly novel operation as far as British tramways were concerned. The unit comprised two of the standard 'D' class four-wheel double-deckers connected permanently together by a rigid bar protected by side guards and lamps to prevent unsuspecting pedestrians from attempting to cross between the cars. One motor was removed from each car, leaving only the two outer axles motored, and the controllers at the coupled ends were also removed. One trolley standard was taken off, and the circuits were rewired so that each controller controlled both the remaining motors.

Though a conductor was still carried on each car, only one motorman was required so the unit made a useful contribution towards easing the staff shortage. Moreover, operating as a single unit, the 'twin' tended to occupy less road space than two separate vehicles, and thus helped to alleviate congestion. It had the advantage over the system of trailer cars (which would have been an alternative arrangement) in that no shunting was necessary at termini – it simply reversed in the same manner as a normal single car. Experience proved that no great difficulties arose in working and no increased danger to passengers. Although the coupled unit proved to be slightly slower than the original single cars (hardly surprising, since it had only one motor per car instead of two) it was stated to be quite able to maintain the not too exacting schedule of the big four-motor bogie cars with which it shared the route, while at the same time its current consumption was lower. Contemporary photographs depict this twin-set filled to overflowing with war workers, and its success inspired the introduction of three more similar units.

Attention was also turned to making better use of the existing fleet of 60 Class C single-deckers which had been supplied by Hurst Nelson in 1901, and 1916 saw the debut of a rebuilt version incorporating the front exit which was to become a standard feature of Newcastle trams and trolleybuses. Originally these long bogie cars had a rear entrance with an adjacent partially-open section especially for the benefit of smokers, and their total seating capacity was 37, with room for another 18 standing. First thoughts suggested the possibility of taking out all the seats to leave an unrestricted space in which to pack as many standees as possible under peak-hour conditions. However, further reflection concluded that something less austere would be more readily acceptable in general daily service, so an internal rearrangement was adopted providing six seats at each end for smokers plus accommodation for 30 passengers on longitudinal seats in the saloon, while still leaving enough room for about 40 standees. Thus the total capacity of around 80 passengers represented an increase of getting for 50% compared with the original version. At the same time the platforms were altered to incorporate a front exit, with the object of speeding passenger flow and easing the task of conductors by ensuring that passengers passed along the car instead of congregating on the rear platform.

A total of 40 of the single-deckers were thus reconstructed with front exit, but some of them later underwent an even more drastic transformation when they became double-deckers. For this purpose, stairways were fitted inside the saloon, leading up to an open-top deck which extended only over the central part of the car; the appearance of this short top protruding above the lower-deck roof soon earned the converted vehicles the name of 'submarines'. The top deck had seats for 28, and this, added to the 38 of the lower deck and some two dozen standing, gave an ability to handle as many as 90 people. The work involved was put at only about £300 a time; this would have given a total cost for converting all 60 cars of £18,000, whereas it was estimated that if the increase in capacity had been met by the purchase of new cars, the cost would have been some £90,000.

The success of the conversions, together with the continuing need to maximise capacity, led to the application of the front exit layout to a new type of double-decker introduced in 1917. This became the standard 'B' class which prospered and multiplied considerably during the 1920s and survived to the final days of tramway operation. The front exit was incorporated not by lengthening the platforms (which would have given excessive overhang) but by shortening them and recessing the stairways into the saloon; the stairways in fact became admirably straight, in contrast to the conventional twisting spiral. The front exit could be closed on the offside by means of a portable door, though later the door became a fixed fitting. Internally, longitudinal seating was provided for 26 on the lower deck, while the upper deck seated 36 in an exceptionally spacious-looking saloon with no internal partitions or bulkheads. The total seating capacity of 62 was slightly higher than on the earlier open-toppers, but with the important advantage that this was an all-weather capacity since the top deck was completely enclosed.

Benefits of the front exit layout were found to include faster loading and unloading, the flow of passengers through the car leading to less congestion and facilitating fare collection. In particular, it was found that safety was enhanced. The number of platform accidents to passengers boarding or alighting was drastically reduced; passengers were unable to jump off before the car had stopped, but had to wait until the car came to a halt and the driver opened the exit door. Moreover, the confusion of passengers getting on and off at the same platform was eliminated. The success of the system in Newcastle prompted its adoption by the Gateshead company, especially in the light of the forthcoming linking of the two undertakings by way of the High Level bridge; it was obviously to the advantage of all concerned if all the cars of the two operators could be of the similar pattern on jointly-worked through routes. So from the start of the 1920s the new Gateshead cars, both single and double-deck, were of front exit layout, though in the case of the double-deckers the design was somewhat different to that of Newcastle: the cars were of more orthodox pattern, and the exit door was arranged under the conventional platform stairway.

Writing after 10 years experience of the front-exit vehicle, the Gateshead company's manager considered 'this type of car as constructed by my company the safest car in use today'. Since it had been adopted, platform accidents had been reduced to 'a very small figure'. Meanwhile Newcastle's manager reported similar experiences: 'Accidents to passengers boarding and leaving the platforms have been practically eliminated'. Sunderland Corporation had also acquired a few front-exit cars at the start of the 1920s, but it appeared to be less enthusiastic about the idea than its Tyneside contemporaries. Here the tradition could have no more sincere recommendation than its perpetuation on Newcastle's new trolleybuses in the mid-1930s.

If these apparently modern ideas of passenger flow and front exit have a respectable tradition on Tyneside, so another of our accepted up-to-date methods has an even longer pedigree. 'Pay-as-you-Enter' was introduced by the Gateshead company as early as 1912, when it became the first operator in Britain to adopt this system on its cars. Several single-deckers were converted by having the platform lengthened and provided with two doorways, one for entrance and the other for exit, divided by a barrier, behind which stood the conductor who collected fares as passengers passed into the saloon.

In the light of our more recent experience with PAYE on our buses, it is interesting to look at the advantages which were then expected to be obtained with this innovation. They were four in number. First, since the conductor would always be on the platform (there was no suggestion of one-man operation at this time) he could better watch over the safety of passengers as they got on or off. Second, it was easier for him to collect fares and to ensure that everyone paid. Third, passengers benefited, since the conductor did not have to enter the saloon to collect fares, pushing through the throng and treading on feet in the process. Fourth, boarding and alighting would be quicker, and thus the service would be improved. An important element in the scheme was the flat fare (in this case 1d) so that fare collection was as rapid as

The big movers: the Newcastle tramcars that shifted the crowds.

Above:
Long bogie single-deckers dated from the earliest years of the electric tramways and were destined for a lengthy life, undergoing substantial rebuilding and modification. In their original form as here they had open end sections with seats for smokers. These 'C' class cars came from Hurst Nelson and had Brill 27G trucks.

Below:
To increase their capacity some of the early single-deckers were later rebuilt as open-top double-deckers, with interior staircases and front exit. From the appearance of the short upper deck they became known as 'submarines'.

Above right:
To cater for heavy workmen's traffic Newcastle operated coupled tramcar sets from 1916 to 1925. Class D four-wheelers were coupled together in pairs, with the inner motor and controller and one trolley-pole removed.

Right:
The open-top 'F' class bogie cars were originally single-deckers from Hurst Nelson in 1901, but were soon rebuilt by the Corporation as 84-seat double-deckers. No 95 is seen at Central station.
C. Carter

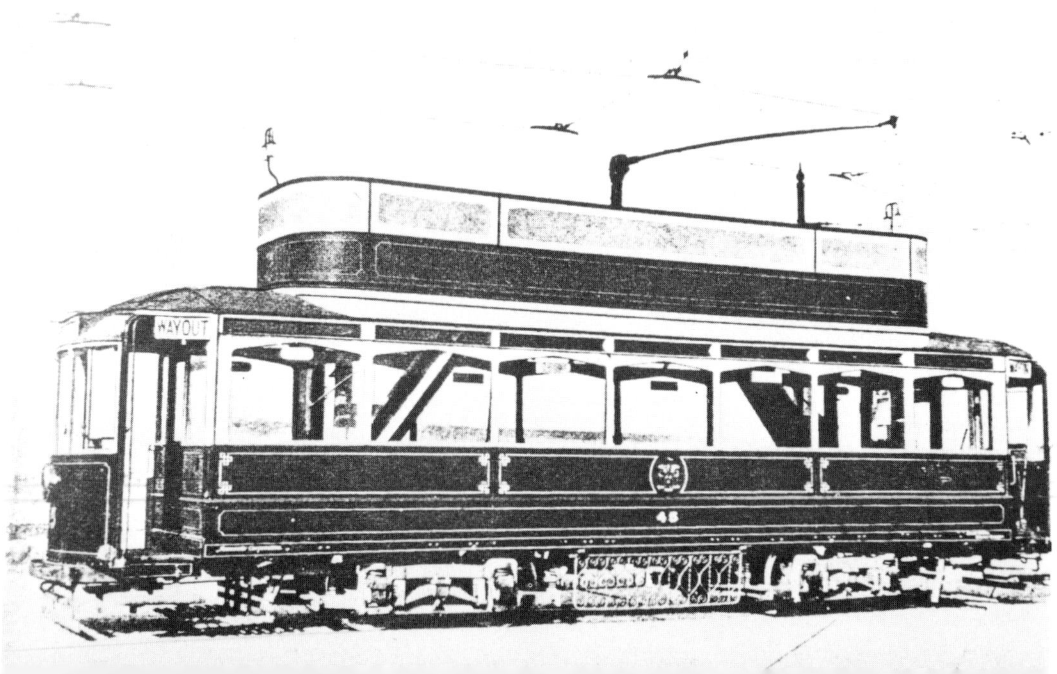

PILGRIM ST
146
146

DEWAR'S THE Whisky
GENERAL
95

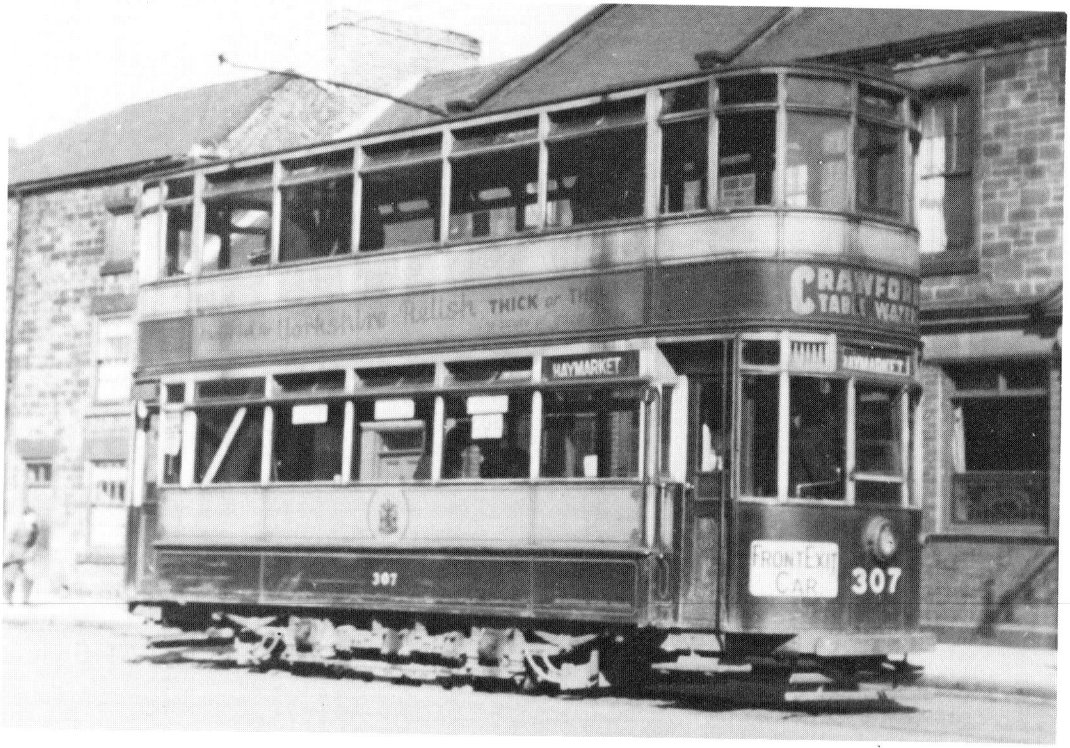
HAYMARKET
THICK or THIN
FRONT EXIT CAR
307
307

VAUX'S STOUT
STOP

Left:
Passenger flow: a comparison in tramcar design on Tyneside between the front-exit double-deck cars of Newcastle Corporation, such as No 307 here *(G. S. Hearse),* and those of the Gateshead & District Tramways Co. The Newcastle example incorporates a straight stairway within the body of the car; the Gateshead vehicle is more conventional, with longer platforms and curved stairways on the platforms and exit arranged beneath the stairs. The prominent 'Front Exit Car' sign and the 'Stop' flag were intended to warn other traffic of passengers alighting from the front end; experience proved that the layout facilitated passenger flow, with increased safety. The standard Newcastle design was built from 1917 to 1926, while the Gateshead car was one of a batch built in 1923.

Above:
Traditional style was maintained when Newcastle Corporation introduced its trolleybuses in 1935, as exemplified on this Karrier with 60-seat Metropolitan-Cammell body with forward exit. *Ian Allan Library*

Tyneside single-deckers.

Below:
A 'Pullman' of Newcastle Corporation; the 'C' class single-deckers had originated from Hurst Nelson as early as 1901, but they had lengthy careers during which they were extensively rebuilt. No 43, seen here at Gosforth in 1946, was one of half-a-dozen rebodied and remotored in 1932–33. It was sold in 1948 to the Gateshead Co where it became No 74.
G. S. Hearse

possible; the now familiar plea to 'have exact fare ready' was already in evidence, reinforced by notices on the car dash proclaiming 'Pay As Your Enter – Have One Penny Ready'.

High hopes were expressed at the official start of the new system. It was hailed as 'the inauguration of a new epoch in tramway undertakings'. On that day, as the managing director of the International Pay-As-You-Enter Tramcar Co (under whose auspices the arrangements had been made) proclaimed, 'for the first time in Europe, cars are being operated under a system which is new in this country, but which is already a household word in the Western Hemisphere'. Tyneside was the pioneer, and 'in days to come, Gateshead would point with pride to the fact that it was the first to recognise the advantages shared alike by the public and the company is pay-as-you-enter'. In the flush of enthusiasm, he can be forgiven for over-optimism. The scheme did not prove as successful as anticipated; while it had been proposed that a front exit should be used, this was not done, and the inadequate space on the platform led to congestion and delay, so the experiment was not widely extended. Nevertheless, he was to be eventually proved right, when the pressure of economic circumstances forced the adoption of PAYE in conjunction with one-man operation on the buses of a later era; but in 1912 the time was not right.

Notwithstanding, the basic concept of the Gateshead company's single-deckers of the 1920s was well in advance of much contemporary practice. Well over 40ft long and mounted on Brill maximum-traction trucks, they had longitudinal seats for 48 passengers, with plenty of room for a good load of standees. Making a virtue of necessity (low bridges limited the use of double-deckers) they had evolved a tradition foreshadowing the present-day high capacity vehicle with its separate entrance and exit and its high standing load. Here again Tyneside was showing the way.

Right:
One of the Newcastle 'Pullmans' sold to Gateshead (No 76, formerly Newcastle 54) stands at Newcastle Central in Gateshead company service in 1950.

Below:
One of the front-exit bogie single-deckers built by the Gateshead company during the 1920s; dating from 1927, No 9 was a 48-seater mounted on Brill 39E trucks.

7 Black-Coated Engines

Nowhere are trade and transport more closely connected than on the North East coast, and to the heavy industries the railway is indispensable – in fact it is easier to get into some of the larger works by river or rail than by road.

R. Bell, Assistant General Manager, London & North Eastern Railway, 1929

Though it was the bright green express engines that caught most of our attention, it was the black-coated goods engines that were earning the North Eastern's bread and butter on Tyneside and Wearside. That faithful workhorse, the 0-6-0, abounded in several varieties. There was the 'P' class, 70 engines built between 1894 and 1898, and the 'P1' class, an enlarged version totalling 140 locomotives built between 1898 and 1902. But the most impressive were the members of the 'P2' class, which bade fair to rival their bigger brothers, the 0-8-0s. The first 'P2' appeared in 1904 with a truly gigantic boiler, claimed to be the largest ever fitted to a six-wheeled locomotive in Britain. With a total heating surface of 1,658sq ft and a grate area of 20sq ft, the 'P2' made an interesting comparison with its contemporary 'T' class 0-8-0 which offered figures of 1,675sq ft and 21½sq ft respectively. The weight of the 'P2' in working order complete with its tender was 83 tons, only some 13 tons less than the 0-8-0. The small wheels of only 4ft 6in diameter served to emphasise the great 5ft 6in diameter boiler towering above them. So successful was the 'P2' that some 50 of the type were soon in service, followed by the generally similar 'P3'.

Great though the 0-6-0s were, the true leviathans were the 0-8-0s of the 'T' class, massive small-wheeled outside-cylindered engines looking capable of shifting anything. And their performance did not belie their appearance; indeed the NER seemed hard put to determine any limits to their power.

In his book MacLean includes a tantalising reference to tests carried out with these 0-8-0s. The report, he tells us, was published in *The Engineer,* so to satisfy our curiosity we searched out the volume for 1901 to read just what did happen on the occasion of these trials. Two of the large pages of that august journal were taken up with a drawing of a 'T' class locomotive and there were several columns of small print. The new locomotives, 'larger and more powerful than anything up to the present made for the NER', were then in service hauling loaded coal trains from Stella Gill, where traffic was concentrated from the nearby collieries, to the shipping staiths at Tyne Dock, a distance of about 11 miles, and of course bringing the empties back. At first the new engines were hitched on to trains of 60 loaded wagons, with a total weight (including a 10-ton brake van) of 985 tons. 'It was found', *The Engineer* records, 'that in spite of a heavy incline and its curvature, this load was handled with the greatest east'. So the train was lengthened until it amounted to 72 wagons, weighing (with brake van) as much as 1,180 tons. Now came the real trial, for one of the locomotives was given a load of 80 wagons plus brake; again this failed to daunt the monster, for 'it accomplished the task with ease', covering the 11 miles to Tyne Dock in 52 minutes.

On another occasion it seems that someone lost count, for by mistake an extra wagon was put on, raising the number to 81, weighing in at 1,325 tons and stretching for 550yd end to end, 'the longest loaded train with which the company had ever dealt'. Even this proved no match for the mighty engine: 'there was such an evident reserve of power that we have no doubt whatever that an even larger load could have been taken', *The Engineer* concluded admiringly. Gradients as steep as 1 in 109 were overcome by 'rushing', the train accelerating on the downhill sections in order to take a run at the incline. The spectacle of some 1,400 tons of train speeding downhill at as much as 30mph, with no other braking available than on the engine and tender and on a solitary brake van swinging along at the tail more than a quarter of a mile away, must have been truly awe-inspiring.

By 1910 more than 70 of the 'T' class 0-8-0s had been put into service, while the modified 'T1' and 'T2' classes went on being built in numbers up to 1921, and a three-cylinder version classed as 'T3' made its appearance in 1919. For many more years these stalwarts were to go pounding on with their lengthy loads of coal and ore.

General goods traffic in Newcastle for long centred on the North Eastern's great Forth Banks depot, although in the early years of the century the old Trafalgar station still received wagonloads of produce such as potatoes and grain, and traffic was also handled on the quayside. But Forth's location made it one of the largest goods stations in Britain. In the early part of our period it was handling well over one million tons a year of merchandise as well as some 800,000 head of cattle. Its total staff numbered about 1,400, in addition to which both the North British and the Caledonian maintained their own agencies at the station. For use in the road distribution of the depot's freight, the stables accommodated 250 horses to trundle the heavy carts through the city streets; mechanisation reduced the number to 100 by 1939, but the last horses were not withdrawn until 1950.

Built between 1866 and 1873, the station was served by lines branching off the Newcastle-Carlisle line to

The NER's sturdy goods locomotives that hauled the coal to the staiths on Tyne and Wear.

Above:
Some 170 of the 'C' class (originally two-cylinder Compounds) were built by the NER between 1886 and 1892, most of them at Gateshead. No 1612, seen here in LNER days as a Class J21, emerged from Gateshead works in 1892. 'They have all been spoken well of by those who have charge of them', MacLean wrote in 1905. *Ian Allan Library*

Above:
At the coaling stage stands one of the NER's 'P' class, of which 70 were built between 1894 and 1898. No 1891 dated from 1896. Note the line of NER coke wagons on the elevated track on the stage.
Ian Allan Library

Below:
The giant 0-8-0s that mastered the heaviest trains to the Tyne: the NER's first eight-coupled engines were those of the 'T' class introduced in 1901 to take 60-wagon trains, though even 70 wagons proved no match for their powers. No 2122 was one of the 1901 batch. *Real Photographs*

A contrast in motive power photographed in the summer of 1946.

Above:
At Tyne Dock, one of the massive 0-8-0s long familiar hauling coal trains to Tyne Dock, 'Q7' class No 633 was formerly a member of the NER's three-cylinder 'T3' class of 1919–24.

Right:
Pausing during shunting operations at Sunderland, 'Y7' class 0-4-0T No 985 was one of the NER's smallest locomotives (and surely the inspiration for many tinplate toy engines). *Ian Allan Library*

Below right:
An 0-8-0 in action: 'Q6' class No 2279 pounds up the grade on a mixed freight in this scene from 1945. *Ian Allan Library*

the west of Central, the main warehouse being sited on a steep bank sloping down to the Tyne. Further extended in 1893, this building was 'constructed more with a view to utility than architectural beauty', a contemporary observer admits, but nevertheless it 'takes the form of an eye-pleasing ellipse'. The slope of the ground allowed the provision of extensive cellars (partly utilised for substantial stocks of beer) while the necessary cranes, capstans and traversers employed in dealing with the wagons were worked hydraulically; the 'accumulative tower' containing the motive power was some 70ft high and something of a local landmark.

Part of the great building had to be cut away to allow for the construction of the new approach lines to Central over the King Edward bridge, while a new goods station had been brought into use at New Bridge Street.

Watch it being built and we would have remarked that there was something distinctly unorthodox about this imposing structure at New Bridge Street. Put in hand in 1904 and completed in 1906 (and destroyed by wartime bombs in 1941), it represented a notable early example of reinforced concrete construction for a large building. Indeed it was claimed to be the first such building designed to carry the weight of moving trains, plus the deadweight of the merchandise, on a concrete floor supported on concrete columns. There was even a spiral staircase made entirely of concrete; of this, the contemporary *Engineer* reassured us that 'although the construction has a somewhat risky appearance to the eye accustomed to masonry work, it is perfectly safe'. Trains were received on two levels, on tracks interconnected by traversers, turntables and hoists, with three storeys of storage space above and offices at one end. A notable feature was an extensive flour and grain store with a capacity of over 2,000 tons, arranged with sloping floor for automatic discharge by way of chutes to the ground floor.

Opened at the beginning of 1907, the new depot was intended to facilitate a division of function with the older Forth depot. New Bridge Street was to concentrate on traffic to and from stations north and east of Newcastle, while Forth would handle traffic to and from the south and west. This would not only speed up despatch and delivery, but would reduce the amount of freight needing to be hauled over the congested tracks through the centre of the city.

The volume of freight carried over the tracks demanded special measures to ensure its smooth operation, and as early as 1917, when wartime conditions had brought practically a doubling of traffic, the North Eastern introduced at Newcastle a system of centralised freight train control. This covered an area extending respectively to Benton Bank Top, Blaydon and Ouston Junction; all freight trains within the area were directed from the control room at Newcastle Central, where three controllers were always on duty.

To say that freight operations got in the way of the passenger trains is perhaps to get our priorities wrong, for the North Eastern was predominantly a freight carrier. Nevertheless there was no doubt that the running of goods trains made it more difficult to fit in an intensive passenger service, and nowhere was this more true than on the north Tyneside electrified lines. In this respect, management was no doubt thankful that at least the Riverside line called for no more than an hourly passenger train, since the tracks had to carry vast quantities of coal to the staiths on the river bank, as well as to the electric power station at Carville and the gasworks at Willington Quay. While the bulk of the traffic turned on to the Riverside branch at Byker, some of it was sent right round the electrified loop via Tynemouth to enter at the east end through Percy Main. Other coal trains came down from the collieries in the Blyth district, and these also had to traverse the electrified lines for part of their journey, while there were collieries on the electric route itself. Much general traffic was also destined to supply the innumerable ships berthing at various docks. In the opposite direction, fish traffic from Tynemouth and North Shields travelled in to be concentrated at Newcastle for onward haulage southwards for the markets of London and other parts of the country.

Electric haulage of local freight traffic might have seemed an obvious step, and at least as early as 1911 the NER was reported to be considering adopting electric traction for goods and mineral working on the electrified lines. But there were practical problems: sidings and yards would have had to be equipped with overhead wires, since the use of the live rail in such locations was ruled out on safety grounds, and working would therefore have involved numerous changeover points as well as dual-fitted locomotives. Such were in fact employed on the only section of electric freight operation on the NER's Tyneside system; two steeple-cab electric locomotives dealt with freight traffic on the Newcastle Quayside line which was electrified as part of the original scheme. In this instance there were special factors which favoured electrification; the mile-long branch not only had fearsome gradients of around 1 in 30, but was mostly in sharply curved tunnels where train working was neither easy for the steam engines nor pleasant for the crews.

Each of the two Bo-Bo electric locomotives for the Quayside branch was fitted with both third-rail collector shoes and a bow collector (later replaced by a pantograph) since the conductor rail was installed only in the tunnel section, with overhead wires in the yards at top and bottom of the incline. Transition from one method of pick-up to the other while the train was moving called for nice judgment by the crew if embarrassing contretemps were to be avoided. The NER may well have been reluctant to interject too many such potential hostages to smooth running.

Quite apart from motive power, coal trains in the area had their own characteristic appearance. Absent were the multitude of variegated private-owner wagons with the names and colours of individual colliery

Coal traffic in the last days of steam power.

Below:
Class K3 2-6-0 No 62024 heads southward past Ryhope Grange Junction with a loaded train from Sunderland in 1964. *M. Dunnett*

Bottom:
Having traversed BR metals from the staiths at Sunderland, National Coal Board 0-6-2T No 10 with empties for Penshaw yard diverges on to the NCB line at Cox Green Junction in 1965. *I. S. Carr*

Stalwart ex-NER goods locomotives were still going strong on their native terrain in the 1960s.

Top:
Ex-'P3' Class J27 0-6-0 No 65892 arrives at Silksworth colliery with coal empties from South Dock, Sunderland, in 1967. *I. S. Carr*

Above:
Ex-'T2' class, 'Q6' 0-8-0 No 63455 approaches Three Horse Shoes crossing on the former Stanhope & Tyne line with a coal train bound for Tyne Dock. The last pre-grouping engines to remain in service, ex-NER 0-6-0s and 0-8-0s continued to haul coal trains until the end of BR steam traction in the northeast in 1967.
I. S. Carr

Above:
The integration of intensive passenger service with heavy freight traffic was nowhere more difficult than on the North Tyneside loop, especially on the busy main line section between Newcastle Central and Heaton. Here an electric train of 1937 stock pulls away from Central and heads for Manors on the loop service. *Real Photographs*

Electric freight power: the two ex-NER electric locomotives of 1904 used on the Newcastle Quayside branch.

Below:
As LNER 6481, locomotive No 2 stands at South Gosforth depot in 1947. *G. S. Hearse*

Above right:
As we might have seen them if local freight services had been electrically operated; pantograph down, No 2 as BR 26501 passes through Heaton station on its way to Heaton depot in 1961. *I. S. Carr*

Right:
Former No 1 as BR No 26500, in the NER-style green livery it was given in 1961 halts at Trafalgar Yard after making its last trip from the quayside on 29 February 1964. Note the changeover from third rail to overhead. The two locomotives had British Thomson-Houston electrical equipment and Brush trucks.
I. S. Carr

companies or merchants such as were seen on the freight trains of most other railways. The North Eastern would have none of that; instead it supplied its own wagons to carry coal from the pits, no doubt to the envy of many other railway companies' officials who cursed the time and labour spent in sorting the numerous private-owner wagons and the dead mileage incurred in returning them empty to their respective homes. Instead the NER maintained a control system, in co-operation with the colliery companies and traders, to allocate wagons to the pits as required.

North Eastern wagons themselves were distinctive. Whereas the 10-tonner for long represented the limit in most parts of the country, the NER was already using 15-ton wagons by the start of the century. Within a few years the 20-tonner was in use, and wagons of this capacity multiplied until they formed the majority of the stock. Even larger vehicles, with capacities up to 40 tons, were employed to take coal from the Ashington collieries to the staiths at Blyth.

Again, while other operators used side or end-door wagons, the NER's wagons were mostly of the bottom-door hopper type, a design adapted to facilitate rapid discharge at the high trestles of the staiths which strode out into the water at Newcastle's Northumberland dock and Dunston, at Tyne Dock and Blyth. A part of the industrial landscape as well as the transport pattern, these tall structures vibrated to the rumbling wagons dropping their coal loads into the holds of waiting ships for export throughout the world. In some places, such as Tyne Dock, gravity was employed to draw the wagons down to the loading point and then to remove the empties to the sidings to await the return journey to the pits.

In the palmy days of the coal trade before World War 1, more staiths were under construction to handle the unceasing flow of wagons. At West Dunston a doubling of capacity was envisaged, more capacity was planned for Tyne Dock, and another million tons was projected at Blyth. The West Dunston staiths were not completed until after the war, and those at West Blyth were not opened until 1928. By this time the tide had turned; the coal trade had slumped, fewer wagons rolled, and the new facilities were doomed to remain under-utilised.

Below:
A reminder of the important part played by the coal trade in Tyne & Wear's transport heritage; Lambton staiths on the Wear at Sunderland. In this 1966 view an NCB 0-4-0ST shunts NCB wagons, while in the distance a 'J27' 0-6-0 heads a northbound coal train over Monkwearmouth bridge. *M. Dunnett*

8 Bridging the Gaps

The adaptation of the High Level bridge for tramway traffic entailed the abolition of the ancient gipsy van-like omnibuses which gave an inconvenient connection between the Newcastle and Gateshead tramway systems. As far as traffic working is concerned the two undertakings are now virtually one.
Tramway & Railway World, 1923

Although the golden years of the tramway boom were over before the start of World War 1, this was not entirely the close of the chapter, for the three municipal operators were still expanding their activities, while the last extension of all was not opened in Sunderland until 1949. Nevertheless, the expansionist years ended with crucial gaps in the network still preventing the full development of through running and interurban services. The tracks of Gateshead and Jarrow were still far asunder, as too were those of South Shields and Sunderland, though in each case there were proposals to link up the lines to create a continuous and unbroken chain all the way from Newcastle, through Gateshead and Jarrow to South Shields and on to Sunderland and beyond. North of the Tyne, Newcastle Corporation and the Tyneside company were engaged in through running between the city and North Shields, though here a physical obstacle was encountered in that the Tynemouth company used a different gauge so that through running to the coast was impossible.

No less decisive in effect was the psychological obstacle apparent in the intractability of adjacent operators when it came to permitting their neighbours' cars to venture on to their tracks. Protracted and sometimes heated negotiations delayed the institution of through services between Newcastle and the Tyneside company, between South Shields and the Jarrow company, and between Sunderland Corporation and the Sunderland District company. Municipal bodies feared the intrusion of outside enterprises which could be the vanguard of the British Electric Traction group's encircling legions intent on establishing a monopoly across the entire region, while the companies scorned the civic dog-in-the-manger attitude which hindered the completion of natural (and profitable) traffic corridors. Whether physical gaps or lack of co-ordination, deficiencies in the network served to hasten the decay of the tramways once the motorbus appeared on the scene. Unconfined to rails and with scant respect for parochial boundaries, the bus in the 1920s was not only to change the basic mode of transport but to transform the scale of operations from local to regional.

'All has ended happily', a relieved *Light Railway & Tramway Journal* was able to comment in 1904 when it reported the agreement between Newcastle Corporation and the Tyneside company. But harmony had not been reached without lengthy argument. The newly-laid tracks of the corporation and the company had met head-on at both Wallsend and Gosforth, but then impasse had ensued; the company not unnaturally wanted to send its own cars from North Shields over the municipal boundary at Wallsend and on into Newcastle, but the corporation did not relish the idea of 'foreign' cars traversing its tracks. The company backed its case with an impressive array of figures to demonstrate how many passengers were inconvenienced by having to change cars at the boundary, how many passengers were lost to both operators because, once having been turned off, they did not complete their journey by car but walked the rest of the way instead, and how many more would in fact be carried by both operators if a through service were offered.

So persistent was the Tyneside company that it sought to obtain Parliamentary powers to enable it to send its cars into the city whether the Corporation liked it or not, a move which the Corporation naturally resented. It was only at an advanced stage of the proceedings that in 1904 peace was achieved as the two bodies agreed on through running arrangements. 'Newcastle Corporation has got rid of the bugbear of compulsion,' the *Light Railway & Tramway Journal* went on, 'and municipalities throughout the United Kingdom have overcome what they feared might have been a dangerous precedent' if the company had been successful in its appeal for compulsory running powers. At the same time, 'The Tyneside Tramways Company have the right of access to a selected point in Newcastle, and an arrangement for the Gosforth traffic which seems likely to meet all the requirements of the case.' In detail, corporation cars were to go beyond the boundary into Wallsend, while company cars were to penetrate municipal territory to provide a through service between North Shields and Newcastle – though, while the corporation permitted the company to use its own drivers, it insisted on having corporation conductors within the city limits. At Gosforth, corporation cars were to be allowed to traverse company tracks beyond the municipal terminus to provide a through service between Central station and Gosforth Park along company tracks which had seemed to block the municipal advance northwards.

Things worked out less happily on the other side of the Tyne, where relations between the Jarrow company and South Shields persisted in being less than

Battlegrounds!

Above:
Wallsend High Street shortly after the coming of the electric cars of the Tyneside Tramways & Tramroads Co. A lengthy legal battle raged before agreement was reached between the company and Newcastle Corporation for the introduction of a through service in 1904. *R. Brook*

Below:
A panorama of Seaburn in 1950: Sunderland Corporation tramcars negotiate the terminal loop while 'Economic' buses approach from Whitburn. Proposals were made for tramway extension beyond the municipal boundary to Whitburn and even to a junction with the South Shields tracks at Cleadon, while for years buses were banned from running along the coastal tramway into the centre of Sunderland.

amicable. A through service between the two towns did start in 1908 after what were described as 'protracted' negotiations, but it ceased in 1911 following disagreement over the distribution of the proceeds. As the historian of Tyneside's tramways, George Hearse, puts it: 'the story of this service was a turbulent one in which bricks of malice and broken bottles of innuendo were hurled across council chambers with singular disregard for the interests of the travelling public.'

The three-mile route of the Jarrow & District Electric Tramways Co was opened on 29 November 1906, in the same year that South Shields Corporation started electric operation. It extended from Western Road in Jarrow, through the town to Tyne Dock, where it made a junction with the South Shields tracks at a spot which acquired a notorious reputation as a bleak and windswept no-man's land peopled by unfortunate travellers perpetually waiting for a tramcar on which to complete their journey.

When the through service started, Jarrow cars worked to South Shields Pier Head, handing over to the corporation all the fares collected on corporation tracks, less a certain sum for working costs; no doubt to simplify the bookkeeping, no through fares were offered, so both passengers and conductors had the extra chore of rebooking at the boundary. A not disinterested observer was the North Eastern Railway. 'If cheap fares are introduced', *Tramway & Railway World* commented with some relish, 'the NER is likely to meet for the first time a strong competition for the very large amount of traffic between Jarrow and South Shields.' The railway fare was 7d return, while the corporation tram fare between Tyne Dock and the Market Place in South Shields was only 1d, so there was ample scope for the new tramway to undercut the railway. The NER could have been excused a smile on its corporate face as it watched the turn of events.

Disagreement over the financial terms of the arrangement resulted in the cessation of the through tramcar service in 1911, only three years after it had started. For more years to come, disgruntled passengers had again to endure the rigours of the Tyne Dock change point. It was not until 1922, after much discussion over the respective merits and demerits of private enterprise and municipal trading, that the through service was resumed, this time with corporation cars taking their share and for the first time running to Jarrow. But amity was short-lived; again dispute arose over the terms of the agreement, and in 1927 the service was again withdrawn, never to be reinstated in tramway days, for only two years later the Jarrow cars ceased to run and were replaced by buses.

Even less success attended the proposals to link the separate systems of South Shields and Sunderland. Plans were put forward as early as 1901 by the BET, but these were quashed by the weight of opposition from the corporations of the two towns as well as from the NER. The two municipalities later produced their own schemes, but were unable to agree upon the route: South Shields wanted to go by way of Cleadon, while Sunderland favoured a line along the coast via Whitburn. The twain were destined never to meet.

Nevertheless South Shields did go on to advance in the direction of its neighbour by constructing a new tramway to Cleadon, reviving optimism that this could be just the first stage in the long-awaited union. We can catch the mood of the time from the words of *Tramway & Railway World*, which saw the extension as 'really only a part of a larger scheme designed to link up Sunderland at Fulwell by a clean sweep across the country, and once on to the Wear, to join a system of tramways which has its ramifications over practically the whole of east Durham.' This latter presumably referred to the Sunderland District company, which extended southward from the town and so would have continued the connection all the way from the Tyne, beyond the Wear and into the Durham hinterland almost half way to the city of Durham itself. Durham County Council also was still nourishing visions of building its own web of lines and might have envisaged its own cars running from Durham to Sunderland, as well as to Chester-le-Street and Gateshead.

The South Shields–Sunderland connection, it was recalled, had 'occupied the attention of the civic heads and departmental chiefs for a great number of years.' Granted earlier schemes had foundered; the BET's plans had succumbed in the face of opposition from the NER. But by contrast, the new plans were in the hands of the municipalities and, said *Tramway & Railway World*, 'that some up-to-date and thoroughly efficient service of through communication will be evolved is regarded as certain.' Admittedly the cost would be high, but the advantages were obvious. 'A through tramway service would not only serve the two populations of Sunderland and South Shields, approximately 300,000, but would tap the large number of intermediate communities in the rural districts into which both boroughs are extending their areas.'

Even if the more optimistic expectations were doomed to remain unfulfilled, the new South Shields extension marked an impressive beginning. The 120ft wide arterial road, built with government aid and hailed as ranking 'as one of the finest in the country', was planned to stride out across the land from one town to the other. At the South Shields end, it ran through Harton to Cleadon under the regal name of King George Road, through a new corporation housing estate under construction on land which had been incorporated into the borough as recently as 1921. The new 1½-mile-long tramway, from the existing route at Westoe, was laid on sleeper track on the central reservation, separated from the carriageways by concrete fencing and privet hedges. This form of construction was cheaper than the normal paved street track and was lower in maintenance costs, while

An important stage in the integration of the Tyneside local transport network was the linking of the tram tracks across the High Level bridge in 1923 to facilitate through running between the tramways of Newcastle Corporation and the Gateshead company.

Above:
Gateshead No 18 emerges from the lower-deck gloom of the bridge on to the Gateshead side. *C. Carter*

Right:
The open lattice structure of Newcastle's Tyne bridge soars above the roadway; bound for Heworth, Newcastle Corporation car No 205 heads across the bridge on one of the new through services into Gateshead in this striking view of 1928. *G. S. Hearse*

Below right:
Not to be outdone, Sunderland built a comparable new bridge across the Wear; constructed around the old bridge so as not to interrupt the flow of traffic, the new Wear bridge was completed in 1929. Here Sunderland Corporation car No 73 enters the town from Monkwearmouth. *C. Carter*

its ballasted sleepers permitted a smoother and quieter ride. And speeds could be higher: Ministry of Transport regulations sanctioned 20mph on the enclosed tracks compared with the maximum of 14mph permitted in the streets.

When this light railway was opened in 1922, the area it served was still only partially developed: as one observer noted, the line simply ended in a field. Only about half the houses being built by the corporation had yet been completed and occupied, although several hundred more were in contemplation. Critics were not backward in condemning the scheme as municipal 'squandermania', while local bus operators, already well entrenched in the district, added their voices in opposition to municipal competition. Nevertheless, early results appeared to offer adequate justification for the new project; a 15min service worked to and from the town centre, and in the first year of operation more than two million passengers were carried. Receipts per car mile reached more than 22d, making this the most remunerative part of the corporation's system. The cars never went beyond their terminus-in-a-field; already in the summer of 1921 Northern General was offering a through service between the two towns. Yet the hope still lingered on, bolstered by hints that the line might be built; the Cleadon tramway survived until 1946, 10 years after the rest of the South Shields cars had succumbed.

When the Cleadon tracks were still being built, news from Sunderland was lending encouragement to those who were looking for the new era of co-operation, for at last agreement had been reached between the corporation and the Sunderland District Tramways, after the lines of the two concerns had stood forlornly apart for some 15 years. In 1905 the company had completed its tracks to Grangetown, where they came within a few feet of those of Sunderland Corporation; but the corporation refused to allow the link-up which would have permitted the company's cars to continue into the centre of the town. So passengers between Sunderland and Ryhope and beyond were obliged to change cars at suburban Grangetown, where often irregular service and poor timetabling interposed irritating delays to travellers. It was not until 1920 that the corporation relented to the extent of joining-up the tracks and allowing the company to run over its lines to the town centre; the new through service started in the new Year of 1921. As if to make up for lost time, some company cars even continued through to the other side of Sunderland to the Sea Lane terminus, while in the other direction corporation cars for a time ventured beyond the municipal boundary to reach Ryhope over company tracks.

The inspiration for this change of heart was only too apparent: motorbuses were on the roads, and by contrast to the tramways, the motorbus showed scant respect for tracks and municipal boundaries. It was quite happy to transcend such niceties and to provide a through service irrespective of the vested interests of tramway operators. Sadly for the tramcars, it was a little too late for repentence, and the new Sunderland partnership enjoyed only a brief life. Never prosperous (it had been in the hands of the receiver within five years of starting operations) the Sunderland District company was plagued by bus competition, and in self-defence it decided to go into the bus business itself. Having decided to dispense with trams, it was already running two dozen buses by early 1925, with more on order, and it withdrew its last tramcars in the same year.

The Sunderland District was one of those tramways which would never have been built if the motorbus had developed 20 years earlier. By the early 1920s track and overhead equipment were in urgent need of renewal, and it estimated that this work would involve an expenditure of well over £150,000; the company just could not afford any such sum. Its dividends took the form not so much of cash paid to shareholders, but rather of social benefits derived from cheap and convenient communications given to the inhabitants of the widely-scattered area it served; such benefits cannot be quantified in money terms, but neither do they bring in the returns needed to maintain a viable undertaking. Moreover, the tramways were at a disadvantage in the face of competition from rival bus operators; if the company could not beat them, then it made good sense to join them, having concluded that 'a motor omnibus service is more in accordance with the tendency of the time'. Whereas the tramcars were confined to their fixed routes, the buses were more flexible and were able to extend over a wider area. Already in 1924 the company had put on its own buses to replace trams between Herrington and Penshaw, and as an indication of the broader scope of the newcomers, the service was extended to Washington. To confirm its break with the past, in 1925 the company dropped the 'Tramways' from its title and instead became the Sunderland District Transport Co.

A glance at a map reveals the disadvantageous position of the tramways. The tracks to Sunderland wandered from Houghton-le-Spring by way of Herrington and Silksworth to Ryhope, before turning northward towards Sunderland (before reaching which, of course, passengers for many years had to change cars at Grangetown). By contrast, the main road, which by this time was alive with the sound of buses, ran in almost a straight line from Houghton to Sunderland along the trunk Durham road. A 'short cut' proposed in tramway days between Silksworth and Sunderland was never built, though ironically the Corporation tracks were later extended to almost within a stone's throw of the former Sunderland District tracks. Further, the tramway's function as a 'feeder' to the railway was also diminished by the growth of interurban bus service; instead of taking the car to Fencehouses station for a train to Durham, or to

Above:
Through running: a car of the Gateshead & District Tramways Co turns into Newcastle's Blackett Street on a cross-Tyne service to Wrekenton. Gateshead car No 27 was one of 25 dating from 1901 and built by the Electric Railway & Tramway Carriage Works on Brill 21E trucks; originally of open-top pattern, they were rebuilt with covered-top decks in the 1920s.
G. H. F. Atkins

Above right:
At the Teams terminus in 1948, Gateshead No 47, in its rebuilt form with enclosed ends and front exit, could boast of almost half a century of service. By now the private car is in evidence, while a Northern General side-engined single-deck bus disappears into the distance on its way into Newcastle; bus services had started before World War 1 to reach areas beyond the tramways. Note the typical BET trolley standard base on the left. *G. S. Hearse*

On the Great North Road in the tramway age.

Right:
Approaching Tyneside from the south, the traveller encounters the tramcars at Low Fell; standing at the terminus ready for its journey into Newcastle is Gateshead & District Tramways No 10 in its shining maroon and white livery. It is the August Bank Holiday weekend of 1938 and traffic is light, though going southward is a modest stream of private cars. The little general store on the right serves as booking office for United and Orange coaches for London and the south.
W. A. Camwell

SHOP AT BINNS
FOR EVERYTHING
TEAMS
FRONT
EXIT
CAR

LOW FELL
WOOLSINGTON GARDEN CITY ESTATE
FRONT
EXIT
CAR

KINGO
TEA

SHOP AT
BINNS'
BINNS
16

Left:
North of Newcastle, the road has already been widened in the 1920s and the tram standards moved from the centre of the road to the sides. Newcastle Corporation car No 1 (one of the 'H' class of 1906–11) reaches Gosforth. Though the private motorcars still have a prewar look, road traffic is already evidently on the increase in this photograph taken shortly after the end of World War 2. *G. S. Hearse*

A day at the races.

Below left:
Well loaded No 16 (one of Newcastle Corporation's 'H' class cars of 1906–11) takes its place in the procession of tramcars along the Great North Road headed for Gosforth Park on a race day in 1946. *G. S. Hearse*

Right:
On the Gosforth Park Light Railway open-top 'F' class car No 106 makes its way through the sylvan setting of the park towards the grandstand. *G. S. Hearse*

Below:
Awaiting homegoing racegoers on the sidings in Gosforth Park are several of the enclosed front-exit cars of the mid-1920s. *G. S. Hearse*

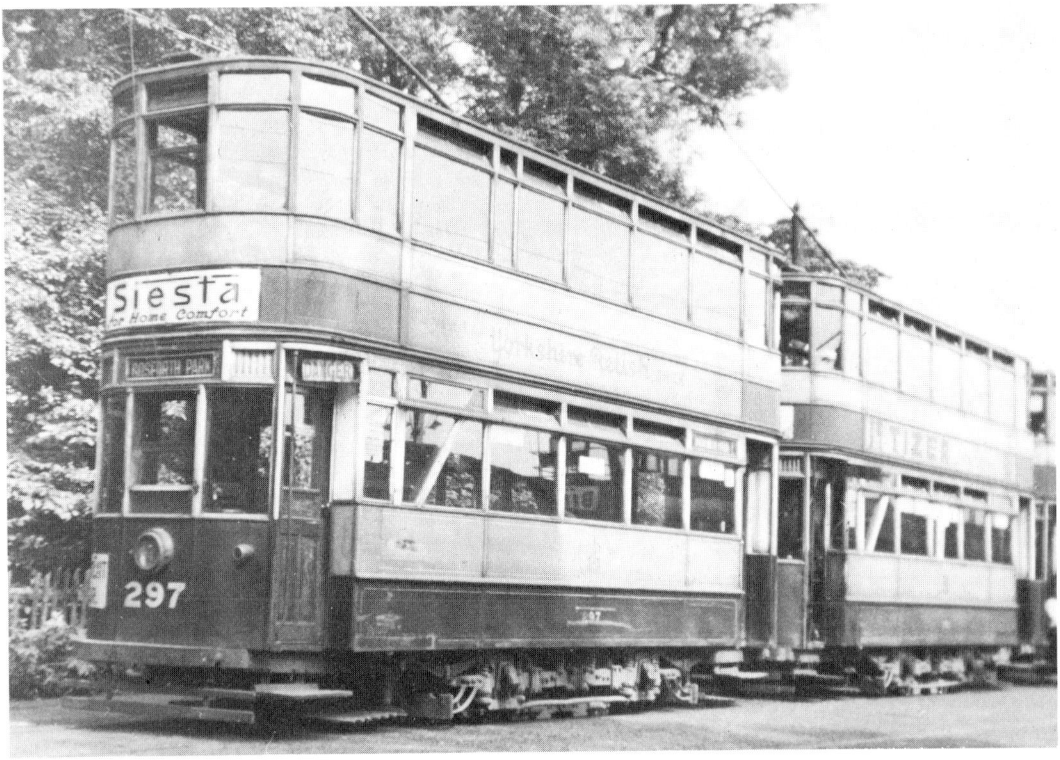

Penshaw for a train to Sunderland or Newcastle, travellers instead boarded a direct bus.

Back on the Tyne, meanwhile, crucial links were being forged at last between the Newcastle and Gateshead tracks. On the face of it, the installation of a tramway across the High Level Bridge to connect the two separate systems was an obvious step – indeed it had been in the air ever since the earliest days of the electric cars. But when it came to the practical details, the connection was not so easy to determine. The owner of the bridge, the North Eastern, was by no means anxious to have other authorities running tramcars across its structure. Partly it was a question of the effect on the bridge itself, which had already been standing since the middle of the previous century; its roadway had not been designed with heavy electric tramcars in mind, notwithstanding that its upper deck was still coping manfully with the massive East Coast expresses that were growing heavier year by year. Partly no doubt the NER's opposition reflected a suspicion that a tramway would abstract business from its own local railway traffic across the bridge. Anyway, the NER went so far as to seek powers to run its own buses across the bridge, though in fact it never did this.

Conscious of the ever growing need for the cross-river link, Newcastle Corporation persisted; it obtained powers in its 1920 Act for such a line, while in 1921 it succeeded in reaching an agreement with the NER. The Corporation would pay more than half the cost of the work needed to strengthen the bridge and relay the roadway, and in addition it would pay the NER a toll of a halfpenny for every passenger carried by tramcar across the bridge. The work was completed at the end of 1922 and, after due congratulation and ceremony, the new line came into use on 12 January 1923. Several through services were introduced, bringing Gateshead suburban termini into direct communication with Newcastle, and lengthy joint workings included a run along the Great North Road between Low Fell and Gosforth. Soon the tracks over the river were carrying some 14 million passengers a year. The horse-drawn omnibuses which had provided the traditional link across the bridge found much of their business gone, but three of them continued at work until 1931, by which time they were probably the last urban horsebuses in Britain.

Nor was this all: the increasing volume of motor traffic during the 1920s was making the High Level bridge quite inadequate, and in 1925 the construction of a new bridge was put in hand. This was the New Tyne bridge, opened by King George V on 10 October 1928. This impressive structure was in effect a 'try out' for the Sydney Harbour bridge then under construction by the same contractors. 'It is interesting to learn', stated our contemporary fount of knowledge, the *Meccano Magazine,* 'that in design and method of construction the new Tyne bridge reproduces, to a scale of about one-third, the immense Australian structure'. The great arch span 'is 531 feet between the centres of the abutment pins, and is the largest arch in the country.' Statistics abounded: the arch rises to a height of 170ft, the roadway is 93ft above high water and gives a clear headroom for shipping of 84ft 6in. The total width is 56ft, with a 38ft carriageway (then carrying a double-track tramway) and two 9ft wide footpaths. 'The bridge has been designed to carry the standard Ministry of Transport load with an ample margin of safety', including the stresses of the frequent tramway service and the heavy industrial traffic; indeed, 'the structure is safe for exceptional loads of 100 tons on four wheels.'

An unwelcome consequence of the new link soon became apparent to Newcastle Corporation. The transport manager reported that the new bridge had led to a considerable decrease in the number of passengers carried on the Corporation's vehicles, since company-operated buses from the south were now encouraged to continue right into the city, instead of terminating at Gateshead and decanting their passengers on to the tramcars. Obviously some adjustment of services was an essential consequence.

The tracks over the Tyne bridge were to prove to be the last new tramway extension on Tyneside. Several new lines had been constructed during the earlier 1920s, mainly to serve suburban housing developments: to the northeast, to Forest Hall and West Moor in 1921, mainly as single track through a still largely undeveloped area; in the same year, from Fenham to Slatyford on sleeper track, with further extension in 1925 and 1926 again on sleeper track to Westerhope, with a branch to Denton Burn.

The construction of these latter sections as roadside sleeper tracks was not only the outcome of economy, but was in line with the current thinking of the Tramways Department. In 1924 Newcastle manager Ernest Hatton had expounded the philosophy of future development; this, he believed, should take the form of track laid on a private road bed. Admittedly this was not often practicable in city areas, but it should be adopted wherever possible for new extensions. Its obvious benefits (which had also been demonstrated on South Shields' Cleadon line) were seen in lower capital costs and lower maintenance costs, smoother riding and higher speeds. He regretted that local authorities had not taken a longer view of the potential of this mode of construction; the traffic needs of an area should always be provided ahead of immediate requirements, as was being done with the Newcastle extensions, in which case it was practicable to undertake the installation of sleeper track tramways at relatively low cost.

The most spectacular of the new lines was the Gosforth Park Light Railway, one of the several extensions planned before World War 1 but not reaching fruition until the 1920s, when a further stimulus was given by the cross-Tyne link with the Gateshead system and the provision of through services. Not only was Gosforth Park a pleasant and popular resort for an afternoon out, but it was also the locale of the racecourse, which was over a mile from the main road and the railway station. Completed in 1924, the new tramway ran through the park, past the grandstand, and included a four-track 'station' to handle the vast race-day crowds. Laid as double track on private right-of-way, the new line was about 1½ miles long, from the Great North Road line at Gosforth, through the park, to join up with the West Moor route, thus enabling 'out and back' services to be run. The delightful sylvan ride savoured of a genuine railway, with embankments, cuttings and bridges, and the 'circular tour' from the city, offering a round trip of about 11 miles for 6d (2½p), was deservedly popular.

Constructed under a Light Railway Order obtained in 1922 by the Corporation following discussions with the Gosforth Park Co, the Gosforth Park Light Railway had involved an expenditure of some £40,000. It remained very much a feast-or-famine kind of route, landing operational headaches on to an undertaking without contributing a steady flow of daily revenue. Race days called for everything that could be put on the tracks, and summer Sundays brought the excursionists, but at other times it was more picturesque than profitable.

A strong hint that some of the extensions of the 1920s were far from a viable proposition, and had only been undertaken under pressure, was given in 1930 by the then manager T. P. Easton. Such extensions, he claimed, had gone ahead because of a government request, in order to provide work for the unemployed. Since 1921, Easton pointed out, the total capital expenditure incurred for these works had amounted to more than £400,000, calling for the sum of over £20,000 a year for interest and redemption charges. If it had been possible at that time, 'to anticipate the wonderful development of other forms of transport', this amount could have been very substantially less. 'The carrying out of some of these extensions has proved unfortunate', he claimed, though in extenuation 'it had been impossible at that time to foresee the rapid progress and development of the petrol omnibus.'

While Easton did not specify which were the 'unfortunate' lines, the fate of some makes their candidature obvious. The short active life of the tracks from Fenham to Slatyford and Westerhope and the branch along Silver Lonnen, gives them a prior claim; their services faded away within a few years. Hardly less sturdy were the claims of Forest Hall and West Moor. Here there were of course the connections with the Gosforth Park Light Railway, but even when the tramways had only a short time to run, the nature of the outer ends of the routes was still distinctly rural; members of the Light Railway Transport League riding the cars in 1946 reported to *Modern Tramway* that 'beyond West Moor the line becomes probably the most picturesque tram route in the country, and a ride along here on a fine day on the top deck of an open-topper is an experience never to be forgotten.' Housing development to bring the needed level of traffic flow had not gone ahead as anticipated, partly owing to the effects of the years of depression, and perhaps partly because of the imperfect co-ordination between transport and planning which manager Hatton had earlier deplored.

9 Buses, Company and Municipal

Success is attending the considerable extension of omnibus services recently made by the Newcastle on Tyne Corporation within and without the city . . . New services lately instituted have given connection to Branch End, Mickley, Prudhoe, Crawcrook, Ryton, Blaydon and other places. Further extensions are contemplated . . .

Tramway & Railway World, 1925

At Whitsun 1912, two Tilling-Stevens petrol-electric buses belonging to Newcastle Corporation plied between the city and Westerhope by way of Barrack Road and Slatyford, carrying about 1,000 passengers a day. So dawned the municipal motorbus era in Tyne & Wear. From the first it looked like being a success; during the holiday a half-hourly service had had to be operated, instead of the advertised hourly headway, and even then the 34-seat open-top double-deckers had been unable to cope with the crowds of citizens anxious to 'enjoy the rural delights of Westerhope', as a contemporary report described the occasion. The fare for the 20min journey of nearly four miles was 3d, but a return fare was offered at only 4d. The Corporation had kept the fares reasonable, the Tramways Committee chairman explained, since 'they hoped to give the people of Newcastle the opportunity of getting into the country, and the country people an opportunity of doing their shopping in the city'. Such was the civic philosophy (a combination of social benefit with sound business sense) behind the corporation's bus policy, which within a few years was to enter upon rapid expansion and thus to find itself in the midst of controversy, for the road of the municipal bus was at times to be a bumpy highway.

Newcastle Corporation was not the only authority expanding beyond the limits of its tracks. As early as 1907 the North Eastern Railway, already in the bus business since 1903, was running a motorbus service connecting the villages of Whitburn and Cleadon with the town and railway station at South Shields; according to a contemporary, this facility immediately gave 'great satisfaction' to the inhabitants of these outlying villages remote from the trains, though complaints were soon made that the heavy vehicles were breaking up the none too substantial road surfaces. Remarkably this motor service started only a few months after South Shields Corporation had inaugurated its electric tramcars, and a worried Corporation sought assurance from the NER that the buses would not undercut its cars within the boundaries. South Shields itself introduced its own municipal buses several years later, when on 30 July 1914 two battery-electric vehicles took up duty; after the war they were fitted with petrol engines.

On 7 May 1913 the Gateshead & District Tramways Co inaugurated its 'Gateshead & District Motor Services' with a route from its Low Fell tram terminus along the main Durham road to Birtley and Chester-le-Street; for this purpose it had taken delivery from Straker-Squire of nine motorbuses, of both single and double-deck types and with a seating capacity of 34. This was the company's response to the demand to provide transport to areas beyond its tracks; extension to Chester-le-Street had been urged by the local authorities concerned, but the company had decided that the cost of laying tracks would not have been justified. If the buses proved a success, it intended to add to the fleet and open up further routes. As it turned out, fortune smiled and services started from the Heworth tramway to Washington and Fatfield, and to Hebburn and Jarrow, and from the Dunston terminus to Swalwell, Scotswood Bridge and Blaydon. So anxious indeed had Hebburn been to welcome the newcomer within its bounds that the District Council had instructed its surveyor to set about mending the main road as quickly as possible; in the opposite direction, Stanley Council had decided to ask the company to run buses into its area.

'The year 1913 will be memorable in the annals of motor traction for the none too rapid awakening of tramway companies to the possibilities of the road motor as a dividend-earning factor', commented *Tramway & Railway World.* It was referring to the formation by the Gateshead, Jarrow and Tynemouth tramway companies of a new bus company, Northern General Transport, for the purpose 'among others, of carrying on and developing in the northern counties transport business in all its branches, including the carriage of passengers and goods by motor vehicles, and of acquiring interests and undertakings carrying on such business'. In particular, its object was to consolidate the road motor interests of the three BET companies, all of which now had an eye on this mode of transport: the Gateshead company was already in business and its sphere of influence adjoined the Jarrow company's territory, while the Tynemouth company had also decided to venture into bus operation. Since the companies were close together geo-

The motorbus era gets under way.

Above:
Newcastle Corporation started motorbus operation in 1912 using Tilling-Stevens petrol-electrics, 'with the idea of providing means of rapid locomotion for the residents'.

Below:
During the 1920s Newcastle Corporation was extending its sphere of influence far beyond its tram termini with buses like this AEC Renown of 1925. 'The manager of Newcastle Tramways is gradually building up his omnibus fleet, and the services in and about Newcastle are popular.' *AEC*

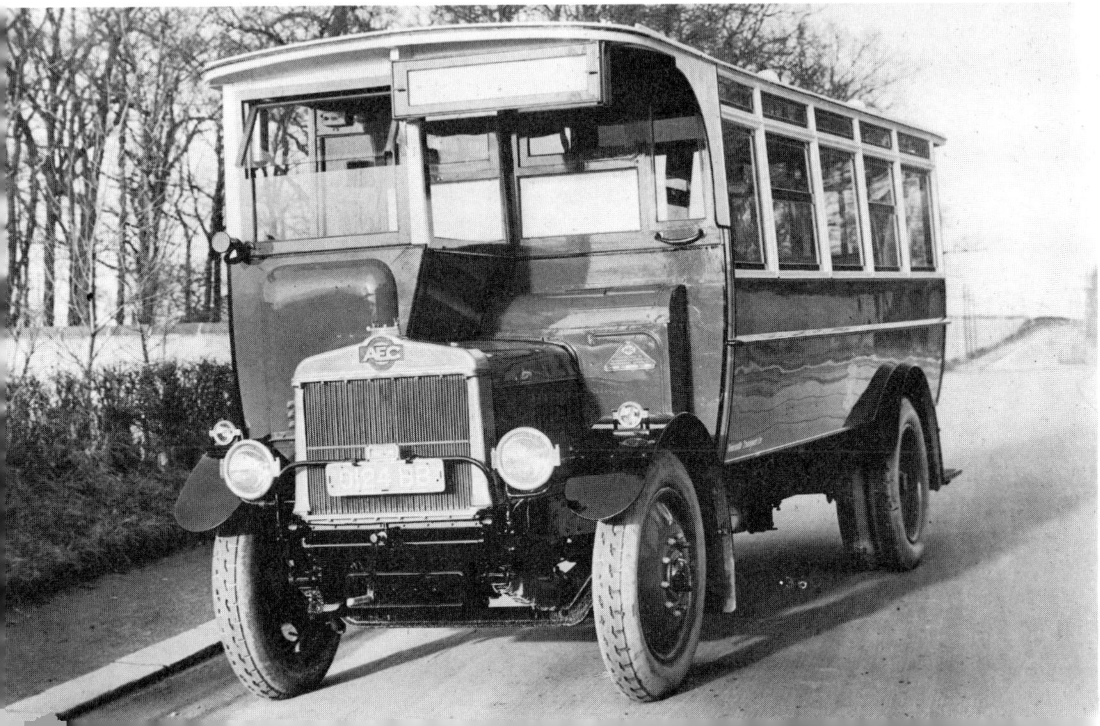

Above:
Northern General meanwhile was employing buses like this Crossley to link mining villages and outlying townships with town and city. 'The new vehicles are fitted with pneumatic tyres . . . The driver is completely enclosed, and the passengers enter by a door at his side.' *Ian Allan Library*

Below:
Representative of the fleet of United Automobile Services in the mid 1920s was this AEC with United-built front-entrance body, one of a hundred delivered in 1926. By this time United's buses were carrying more than 30 million passengers a year.
Ian Allan Library

graphically, the development of separate services by each looked like leading to problems of overlapping, while the successful exploitation of the great potential of the motor vehicle was seen to demand considerable capital expenditure as well as expertise and organisation; this it would be the object of Northern General Transport to provide. Gateshead & District's brief first career as a bus operator was thus terminated at the start of 1914 when its vehicles were transferred to Northern General, which by the outbreak of war later that year found itself with a fleet of more than 50 vehicles.

Wartime conditions brought a temporary halt to developments; buses were requisitioned and staff taken for military service, and Newcastle Corporation was even obliged to use converted lorries to transport mine workers. But the real battle was joined during the early 1920s when the modern bus established itself on the inter-town routes under the enterprise of both large and small operators. In 1922, for example, we read that Northern General 'have placed in service six Daimler saloon omnibuses, accommodating 20 passengers. The new vehicles are fitted with pneumatic tyres. The driver is completely enclosed, and the passengers enter by a door at his side.' Better roadside facilities were also improving the lot of the traveller; at the Low Fell interchange, the company arranged for a station with a waiting room, making the best of the situation where country buses had to stop where the tram tracks began, a situation foreshadowing the later accepted concept of road/rail co-ordination, albeit for different reasons. By 1923 Northern General was operating no fewer than 17 regular services from Chester-le-Street alone; it had also diversified into the coaching trade, offering tours to Yorkshire, the Lake District and Scotland with its 'large fleet of well-appointed vehicles'.

A major protagonist in the bus business was United Automobile Services, a great octopus of a combine which, originating in East Anglia in 1912, spread itself over most of northeast England. Services had begun around Bishop Auckland in 1912, and then in the early 1920s much activity occurred in Northumberland with the company established in Newcastle by 1922. The old solid-tyred buses gave way to modern Daimlers on pneumatic tyres, with the latest style of front-entrance bodywork emanating from the company's Lowestoft works. As well as Newcastle, they served Sedghill, Seaton Delaval, Cramlington and Blyth, North Shields and Whitley Bay, and as far north as Ashington and Morpeth. A new depot to accommodate 140 vehicles was built at Jesmond at a cost of £40,000, and at the start of the 1930s the northern district offices were transferred there from their old location at Blyth. In 1929, by which time the fleet numbered more than 600, United was acquired jointly by Tilling and British Automobile Traction and the LNER, though only after much negotiation and many offers and counter-offers, for the LNER desired to obtain a control which would lessen the element of competition between road and rail. From the New Year of 1930 three formerly separate operators, Robert Emmerson, Eastern Express Motors and Reliance Motors (in all of which the LNER had an interest), were merged into United, and the LNER, inheritor of the long tradition of the North Eastern, gradually faded out of direct bus operation.

The LNER also acquired an equal share with the BET in Northern General, whose fleet had grown from 170 vehicles in 1925 to around 350 by the start of the 1930s. A new garage in South Shields was completed by the beginning of the new decade, while in Sunderland a depot had been opened in 1924 and the local 'Invincible' company acquired in 1925 to give a service to Seaham Harbour. Nearby, negotiations had begun in 1926 with the ailing Sunderland District company; however, replacement of the tramcars by a batch of Leyland Lions had proved so financially encouraging that it was not until 1931 that Sunderland District finally yielded and came under the control of Northern General. After this, although Sunderland District's blue buses retained their separate identity, the routes of the two concerns became, as Charles Dunbar has put it, 'completely mixed up', so that often one did not know whether to expect a blue bus or a red one. Another acquisition, in 1929, Wakefields Motors of Percy Main also retained its old name.

Much of the story of the big concerns was thus the process of enlargement by the taking over of smaller concerns, but a number of independent operators were to survive for a long period. 'Economic' started in 1925 with a service between Whitburn and Sunderland's Sea Lane tram terminus. After numerous vicissitudes involving the usual problems of licensing to obtain access to municipal preserves, as well as competition from other operators, services were extended to both South Shields and the centre of Sunderland. Another long-lived operator, Venture Transport, could trace its ancestry back to 1912 when an open second-hand bus started to run from the Bensham tram terminus to the outlying villages of Whickham and Burnopfield. Various amalgamations led to the formation of a new company in 1938 and this grew to become the largest independent operator in the area. From Newcastle, services were established up the valleys of the Tyne and the Derwent, to reach points as far scattered as Consett and Shotley Bridge, Crawcrook and Prudhoe, Blaydon and Newburn. Prominent among the fleet in the immediate prewar period were a batch of Albion Valkyries with smart Willowbrook bodies sporting the 'rising sun' emblem. Such names among many others deserve their place in the annals of the area's transport history as pioneers of individual initiative, maybe out of harmony with the established operators and the municipalities but bringing their own brand of enterprise in serving many an isolated commuity and so enhancing the quality of life for many folk.

Between South Shields and Sunderland.

Above:
One of the denizens of the coast road during the 1930s, this Albion Valkyrie M65 with 32-seat Alexander body, supplied to Ted Wilson of Whitburn, one of the partners in Economic Bus Services, took up its duties in 1932. Economic survived until acquired by Tyne & Wear Transport in 1975.
Ian Allan Library

Right:
Northern General had been working on a Sunderland–South Shields service in the early 1920s, and some 10 years later this front-entrance Short-bodied AEC Regent of 1933 was photographed in operation as local patrons posed for the cameraman on an obviously dismal day. Note the 'Bus Halt' sign. Like other members of the fleet, No 574 was later given a rear-entrance body. *AEC*

Independents in Newcastle.

Above:
In its smart brown, red and cream livery, one of the AEC Regals of E. Howe of Spennymoor, the smaller of the two operators which comprised OK Motor Services, leaves Marlborough Crescent bus station for Bishop Auckland in 1948. *C. Carter*

Left:
Standardisation in the Venture fleet; No 146 was one of 60 Daimler CVD6s with 35-seat Willowbrook bodies, obtained between 1946 and 1948.
Ian Allan Library

Below left:
Venture Transport No 125, another of the fleet of Willowbrook-bodied Daimlers, departs from Marlborough Crescent in 1948 on route 33 for Rowlands Gill and Chopwell. Venture was acquired by Northern General in 1970. *C. Carter*

On the municipal side, Sunderland Corporation was a latecomer to the realms of motorbus working, much to the subsequent regret of manager Charles Hopkins. The Corporation did not obtain the necessary powers until 1927, and it was 1929 before the first of its Leyland Lions were on the road. When the tram route to the docks was withdrawn on 6 February 1928, Northern General buses had to be used in replacement since the Corporation did not yet have any of its own available.

But if Sunderland lagged, Newcastle Corporation more than made up for it, setting its bus sights on distant horizons during the 1920s. Armed with its newly acquired powers to run buses widely in both Northumberland and County Durham, from 1920 onward Newcastle sent its buses far beyond the municipal boundaries, finding a gratifying welcome from the residents of outlying townships and villages, if not always from the respective local authorities in the areas concerned. A proposal to run buses from the tramway at Scotswood Bridge across the Tyne to Blaydon and Ryton soon brought a request from the mining villages of Crawcrook and Mickley for the service to be extended there; Durham County Council, however, was more cautious and wanted to know how much the Corporation was willing to pay to maintain the roads under the pounding of the heavy vehicles. Nevertheless, in the summer of 1921 corporation buses were running to Crawcrook, Ryton, Wylam, Prudhoe, and Mickley, the end of the nine-mile route offering access to the local beauty spot of Stackfield where city folk could enjoy the country air. The fare for the journey was 1s 3d (about 6p). Road maintenance remained a ticklish question; it was not long before Ryton Urban Council suggested that the corporation should use smaller and lighter vehicles running on pneumatic tyres, since the weighty solid-tyred buses were damaging the roads and causing uncomfortable vibrations in the adjacent houses. To this Newcastle Corporation replied rather unfeelingly that if Ryton Council kept their roads in better condition, then much of the cause for complaint would be removed.

Newcastle meanwhile had agreed a formula with another of the local authorities into whose area it was venturing. Newburn Urban Council in 1921 agreed to let the Corporation's buses operate a route through North Walbottle and High Callerton to Ponteland, a distance of some 10 miles from the city, on condition that it was paid an annual sum equivalent to 1d per mile run.

Success for the municipal buses seemed to be instant. In 1922 Newcastle's manager was able to report that for the past year his buses had carried well over 2 million passengers, after carrying some 1¾ million in the previous year, while receipts had risen by a healthy 50%: from £20,000 to more than £30,000. Now to the coast at Seaton Sluice, or up the valley of the Tyne to Hexham, through mining village or potential suburb, all looked fair ground for the corporation's blue single-deckers.

As the corporation saw it, the role of the bus was to bring an increasingly extensive region within easy access of the city, with all the benefits that could mean: from big town shops to delight the rural housewife (and attract more trade to city shopowners, who were of course ratepayers and so interested in the results of the municipal transport undertaking) to pleasure trips to seaside or country on a Sunday or holiday. The bus was not intended to compete with existing tramways – far from it. Generally it ran outward from the suburban tram terminus without entering the city proper at all, in order to avoid paralleling the tracks and taking traffic away from the cars. If one came in from Seaton Sluice, the bus stopped at West Moor where the passengers were evicted to complete their journey into the city by tramcar. In cases where dual running could not reasonably be avoided, some protection (and some disincentive to the passenger) was given by charging an extra ½d on the bus fare.

The scope of the municipal bus system had been outlined by Newcastle's manager Ernest Hatton when the corporation was seeking powers in its 1920 Bill. The bus routes, he explained, aimed at linking outlying villages with the tramways; the proposed extension to Heddon, for example, would be the means of enabling the residents of that town to make use of the tramway to reach the city. He was no less convinced of the need for services to such seaside resorts as Seaton Sluice or Whitley Bay. While the day of the tramway had not yet ended, the motorbus was the only means of serving the less densely populated districts. He pointed out that the mining villages in the Newcastle area were in a constant state of development; to meet this growing demand, instead of having to seek separate powers for every new bus route, it was much more logical for the corporation to have the general power to put on a bus route as and where it considered desirable.

Expansionism not unnaturally provoked reaction from those not entirely in sympathy with Newcastle's policy. In 1926 the Corporation promoted a Bill to give it widely extended omnibus powers, including powers not only to run on any existing tram route but on other routes way beyond its boundaries to the extent of 21 miles from the city. Such powers were needed, according to Alderman Mayne, chairman of the Transport Committee, in order to develop the system 'in accordance with the needs of the times' which called for a much broader outlook. He deplored the 'ring' which the Ministry of Transport had put around Newcastle, apparently with no regard to the impact of such a limitation.

The question of licensing aroused some feeling. While Newcastle corporation as the local licensing authority possessed powers to license buses running within its boundaries, it could use these powers to prevent the intrusion of outsiders into its territory. To

Newcastle Corporation's 'Blue Buses' in action: two scenes from about 1930.

Above:
In Percy Street, the crew are engaged in starting their charge, an AEC Regent of 1930 vintage with stylish Hall Lewis body featuring sliding windows on the upper deck and an unusual 'porthole' window under the open stairs. 'An improved type of semi-bucket seat is installed. On fine days any amount of fresh air is available, for the lower saloon windows include on each side two drop windows . . . The driver's cab has a coach-type entrance door.' At this time most of the bus fleet still consisted of single-deckers, and two examples are just visible. *AEC*

Below:
Passengers bound for High Heaton climb the open stairs of Newcastle Corporation No 100, another Hall Lewis-bodied Regent, in this animated scene in Northumberland Street. Note the stop sign lettered 'Blue Bus Stop' on the refuge island; also on the left a hint of coming private car competition for the city's street space and its public transport. *AEC*

protect its own services – both tram and bus – such powers seemed a logical system. But, its critics countered, was it reasonable that, having refused to allow outside operators access to its own area, the corporation should then be permitted to push its own buses beyond its boundaries to compete with those very operators to whom it had shut its gates? Such a situation was branded as 'an illogical absurdity.'

Lined up with the opposition was the railway company, where no doubt longer memories recalled the tramway competition which had prompted the electrification scheme of some 20 years earlier. Now buses could eat further into local traffic on other lines if the corporation achieved its aim to send its buses to such places as Ryton, Heddon and Blaydon. On the electrified lines, Whitley Bay would also be under attack; however, another interested opponent, the Tynemouth & District Tramways, ridiculed the idea that anyone should choose to go from Newcastle to Whitley Bay by bus when there was a perfectly good train service which took you there in less than half an hour – why, the bus would take at least 1½ hours to do the 12 miles! Nevertheless it too was concerned that municipal buses would compete with its coastal tramway. It was later to find that many people would indeed take to the bus for the ride to and from the coast, a route on which tension was to run high at times among the various operators involved.

Meanwhile the NER raised one of the long-standing objections to municipal trading: that it was backed by the security of the rates, which therefore presented it with a bottomless purse from which it could subsidise any non-profitable project for any length of time at the expense of the long-suffering ratepayers. It was thus not bound by the limitations of profit or loss which a self-respecting commercial company had to obey. Whether municipal undertakings were in fact run on this basis was open to question; certainly as far as Newcastle was concerned, the answer had been given before World War 1 by Alderman (then Councillor) Mayne as vice-chairman of Newcastle's Tramways Committee: 'every development should be such as will yield to its sharedholders, the ratepayers, a profit on their investment.' The term 'profit' he admitted need not be in the form of cash; it could equally well be in social benefit in the form of a service provided to open up a new and healthier area for housing development. It was probably on this basic definition that municipal trading differed from private enterprise. However, Newcastle's bus division was able to turn in some useful cash profits: a net profit of more than £12,000 in 1926 when some 6 million passengers were carried, and nearly £6,500 in 1930 when the 70 vehicles running on 70 miles of routes carried more than 11 million passengers.

By the middle of the 1920s the city's buses were being extended farther and farther into the surrounding hinterland: from Ponteland to Belsay to give a route of 15 miles from the city centre, and along the banks of the Tyne through Blaydon to Ryton, Crawcrook, Prudhoe, Mickley and Branch End, and through Heddon-on-the-Wall to Hexham. The vehicles were now far removed from the pioneers of a decade earlier; Dennis, AEC and Guy chassis ran on pneumatic tyres, with 28-seat rear-entrance saloon bodies by Strachan & Brown, and Daimler CM-type with both front and rear door bodies came from the United Automobile works at Lowestoft. By the end of the decade several of the new AEC Regents had appeared with 50-seat open-staircase bodywork.

Though everything seemed to be rosy, unrestricted competition was being blamed for the loss of many thousands of pounds a year to the municipal undertaking. Much of it was 'legal' competition, the result of agreement with outside operators to license their vehicles to run within the city boundaries, but much was 'illegal' competition from unlicensed private operators. While (until the Road Traffic Act of 1930) the corporation was the licensing authority for its own area, the amount of control was often greater in theory than in practice, and the corporation had its hands full in trying to cope with the situation. The extent to which this was practicable was illustrated by the case of one particularly persistent 'pirate' who had been summonsed more than 70 times for 'plying for hire without a licence'; he had paid a total of about £120 in fines (no doubt accepted philosophically as an 'operating expense', and an indication of the profitability of the trade) but the proceedings had cost Newcastle Corporation more than £750, and still apparently without achieving the desired result.

If any routes crystallised the tangled mesh of co-operation and competition and of municipal and company attitudes, it was those between Newcastle and the coast. Here was a naturally well-established traffic 'corridor' along an almost completely built-up area comprising residential, industrial and seaside districts, out through Byker and Walker, to North Shields, Tynemouth and Whitley Bay. Early in the century, as we have seen, tramcars had traversed the ground, and after a period of skirmishing an agreement had been reached on through running between Newcastle Corporation and the Tyneside Tramways company. Now the development of the motorbus and the Tyneside company's growing attachment to the new mode, coupled with civic thoughts that the corporation might purchase the company and so extend its sphere of influence to the coast, produced a lengthy period of confusion, full of negotiation and counter-negotiation, agreement and disagreement, leading to an uneasy compromise on sensitive subjects such as services, fares and the number of vehicles to be employed by each participant. The matter was further complicated by the appearance of new private operators anxious to take their share of this lucrative main line, while on the sidelines the railway company (already hedging its bets by taking a stake in bus

Co-ordination on the road to the coast.

Right:
Still following imaginary rails! This 1932-vintage Short-bodied AEC Regent of Northern General's associate Tynemouth & District on the Tynemouth–Whitley Bay route seeks to perpetuate the memory of the trams it has recently replaced. The destination indicator reads 'Whitley Bay via Tram Route'. *AEC*

Below right:
At Newcastle's Haymarket bus station in 1947; Weymann-bodied AEC Regent II of Wakefields Motors (a Northern General subsidiary since 1929) leaves for Tynemouth on joint service 11. Note that while there is a roller blind indicator for the route number, the destination is shown by a board by the lower-deck front window. Also visible in the picture are a United Leyland single-decker bound for Ashington and a Newcastle Corporation double-deck Daimler. *AEC*

Below:
By the early 1950s some 150 buses an hour were leaving Newcastle's Worswick Street bus station at peak time. In this 1954 view can be seen a United Bristol (extreme right), then four Northern General Guy double-deckers with, between them, a Sunderland District Leyland Royal Tiger and a Northern General Tiger Cub. Destinations served include Darlington, Easington, Heworth Colliery, Durham, South Shields and Marsden. *G. H. F. Atkins*

undertakings) looked to means of holding its own customers.

At one time Newcastle Corporation had come close to buying up the Tyneside company. In the mid-1920s a price of almost £120,000 had been set on the undertaking with its 17 miles of tracks and 30 cars, and the city looked destined to achieve its eastward advance. But it still needed to obtain the necessary statutory powers, as well as the approval of the local authorities concerned to permit its vehicles to traverse their streets. But, jealous of the creeping hegemony of their big neighbour, and with the seductive thought in mind that they themselves might indulge in their own municipal transport operations, both Wallsend Corporation and Tynemouth Corporation cast dubious eyes on Newcastle's plans. Nor indeed did the city's ratepayers appear enamoured of the idea, and in the event the purchase never took place. The company went its own way and replaced its trams by buses (the last cars ran on 6 April 1930), but these in turn brought more headaches for the corporation when the company wanted to run them along the corporation's tramways into the city. The company, which had not paid a divident since 1922 (probably a fact not unnoticed by interested parties contemplating a takeover) obtained powers in 1930 to abandon its tramways, parts of which in Wallsend and Gosforth would pass to Newcastle Corporation for incorporation into the city system, while agreement was reached for the new buses to run into corporation territory from Wallsend to the city centre.

Some complication was added by the ambitions of next-door Tynemouth & District, now itself a bus operator and keen to extend its activities beyond the confines of its old tram tracks. The company objected to the joint working between Newcastle and the Tyneside company and was not happy until it too was granted licences to run its own buses into the city. Three years earlier the Ministry of Transport had upheld Newcastle's decision not to issue licences to the Tynemouth company for extending its Monkseaton–Wallsend service into the city; although the difference in track gauge had kept the tramcars out, the buses suffered no such impediment. Official support for the rejection had given heart to the municipalities in their fight to keep outside competitors from their territory, but now it looked as though the walls could no longer be held.

Extra impetus to the bus service had come with the completion in 1927 of the new Coast Road, which effectively shortened the journey between city and seaside. A new highway about eight miles long, the Coast Road connected Newcastle with Tynemouth through Longbenton, Heaton and the north of Wallsend, so by-passing the old congested road followed by the tramway through the centre of Wallsend and North Shields. Originating at the instigation of Wallsend as part of that borough's town planning scheme, it was adopted as a measure to relieve unemployment, and the Ministry of Transport met half the cost of the work. As built, the new road had a 30ft carriageway, with tree-planted grass verges and footpaths, and sufficient land was available for eventual widening to 102ft. A proposed extension from Billy Mill to Whitley Bay had however not been carried out, so traffic for the coast continued to be funnelled through narrow streets at the Tynemouth end of the Coast Road, but nevertheless the effect was immediate. As far as bus services were concerned, Newcastle and Tynemouth corporations agreed that Newcastle should have the disposition of 60% of the licences and Tynemouth the remaining 40%. The new direct way abstracted through passengers from the old established route, and caused more hard thinking for the railway in the face of a rival offering a more competitive service.

Indicative of the new motorbus era was Newcastle Corporation's approval in 1928 for the provision of bus stations in order to allow services to be properly coordinated, so that passengers could make connection between the growing number of both suburban and interurban buses at convenient centres rather than a succession of busy streets, where moreover the multiplying vehicles were adding appreciably to congestion. The bus station at Marlborough Crescent, with nine platforms for both company and municipal buses, was brought into use in 1931, though not before the corporation had needed to persuade the companies that the charge for the use of the new facilities was worthwhile compared with free parking in the streets. So in Marlborough Crescent were to be seen not only corporation buses but also the vehicles of Northern General, United, Emmerson and the General County Omnibus Co.

By the 1950s Newcastle's three main bus stations had become, in the words of the city engineer's department, 'grossly inadequate'. In peak periods more than 100 buses left Haymarket in the course of one hour, while Marlborough Crescent and Worswick Street each handled some 150. Although thought had been given to the possibility of concentrating the load on to a single central station, this idea had been rejected, and the existing three stations had been retained and included in the city's development plan.

10 Protection and After

If nothing short of a monopoly can secure to the community a self-sustaining and efficient service, then, on broad grounds of public policy and in the public interest, we place our claim as high as that of a monopoly.

Alderman Richard Mayne, Chairman, Newcastle Corporation Transport Committee, 1922

Before the end of the 1920s Newcastle's Tramways Committee had already made clear its policy of protectionism: to open up new routes to serve new housing development, the motorbus would be adopted, offering fares similar to those on the tramcars. Where such a route 'traverses or competes with a tramway', however, the fare would be ½d above the tram fare. This was to give 'protection' to the tramways, though necessarily at the expense of those who did not use them; how far such a policy could be considered equitable could be open to question. It could be an argument in favour of the corporation's agreed policy that the tramways should be withdrawn as the occasion arose, whereby the anomaly could then be removed. Such 'protection' could also do little to smooth the feelings of private bus operators, who – perhaps refused a licence by the corporation to run their buses, at fares which they could offer below those on the municipal services – might have been reminded of the old fable of the dog in the manger.

The advent of the Road Traffic Act of 1930 was hailed as the answer to the evils of both protectionism and unrestrained competition. Stricter control would be enforced by the creation of the Traffic Commissioners with powers to license bus services and to attach conditions to such licences, while high standards of fitness would also be enforced on the vehicles in the interests of safety. Now, instead of the various local authorities acting as licensing authorities (however effectively or otherwise this power may have been functioning) all buses both company and municipal had to be licensed by the Commissioners, who would have due regard to the need for the service and the interests of the public.

Under the new regime, established operators might look forward to a more peaceful life free from the incursons of 'pirates' nibbling away at their traffic, although some were concerned that the Commissioners might not view their position in quite the same light as they did themselves. Newcastle Corporation, for example, wondered if the Commissioners would take a different view of its policy of protection. Along with other municipal operators who faced the same problem Newcastle made sure that its case was put to the Northern Area Traffic Commissioners, and was relieved when its submissions met with a sympathetic response.

In 1931 the Commissioners accepted the principle of protection: in cases where a bus service paralleled a tramway, it would be a condition of issue of a licence that the bus fare should be higher than the corresponding tram fare. Such a concession, they stressed, was intended only to protect 'an efficiently worked and economically managed tramway system, capable unaided of affording at all times adequate service to the public dependent upon it.' Similar protection would also be given on trolleybus routes. But what happened in cases where a tramway was replaced by motorbuses? The Commissioners admitted that this question had caused them 'considerable anxiety', but they eventually came to the conclusion that in general protection should also apply here, but with the proviso that fares should be no higher than on the tramcars.

How the principle of protection worked in practice was demonstrated on Newcastle's trunk Great North Road route. The Traffic Commissioners rejected the corporation's plea for a ban on private buses picking up or setting down passengers on the tramway between the city centre and Gosforth, but fixed the minimum bus fare at 3½d instead of the previous 3d and disallowed any concessions on return fares – previously a 5d return had been issued. Those passengers therefore who were misguided enough to choose to travel by bus – either because they preferred a shiny new vehicle with upholstered seats instead of wooden ones and perhaps less crowded, or because the bus made fewer stops and was faster than the tramcar – were thus obliged to pay extra for their discrimination. How long such a distinction could be socially justified was one factor to be taken into account in assessing the future of the tramways.

Meanwhile the application of the Commissioners' principles to the running of municipal buses beyond their own boundaries, to provide services into neighbouring districts or between town and town, was also effectively delineated in 1931 when several operators put in such claims. The Commissioners made it clear that they were not prepared to offer protection to municipal vehicles outside their own territory; in such instances they would have to accept equal terms with private operators. They told Newcastle that the general principle of protection would be applied to the tramway routes within the city to the extent that a penny extra could be charged for each stage where a corporation bus paralleled a tramway, while as far as private operators were concerned they would have to charge a minimum of 3d for any journey made within the city limits. However, protection could not be given to a

Right:
A striking front end look at one of Northern General's advanced side-engined single-deckers of the 1930s. This is No 820, one of the 1938–39 batch with 40-seat English Electric bodywork. *Ian Allan Library*

Below:
This nearside view of another member of the same class (No 822) shows the front entrance and the smooth lines of the body design. Note the difference in front-end styling between the two vehicles. The type 'has quickly proved its usefulness in dealing with traffic during rush hours, thus reducing the number of duplicate vehicles required', reported *Transport World.*

Development of the more conventional Northern General single-decker is exemplified by these two pictires of prewar and early postwar designs.

Above:
AEC Regal No 905 dated from 1937; it has the characteristic low-slung headlamps and large single indicator. *AEC*

Below:
Photographed when new in 1949, Guy Arab No 1256 has a 38-seat Brush body with sliding windows and the noticeable curved front to the cab.
G. H. F. Atkins

SHOP AT BINNS
WHITLEY BAY
AFT 53

S.C.T.
TOWN
83
GR 9114

By bus across the Tyne and the Wear.

Left:
Passing over the Tyne Bridge on a rainy day in 1958. this Leyland Titan PD2/12 with Willowbrook body was one of five which had recently been placed into service by Tynemouth & District. *Ian Allan Library*

Below right:
Just coming off Sunderland's Wear Bridge is the corporation's new No 83, a Roe-bodied AEC Regent III. The absence of road traffic in this 1947 scene is noticeable. The railway bridge is visible on the left. *Ian Allan Library*

Right:
Loading in the city in 1946, Newcastle Corporation AEC Regent No 28 sports the postwar style of blue livery with modernised lettering on the indicator blinds. *AEC*

Below:
Newcastle Corporation's postwar replacement fleet included numbers of Leyland-bodied Titans, such as No 6 seen here at the Haymarket terminus in 1954. *G. H. F. Atkins*

municipal tramway which extended beyond the boundaries, or to any such route on which buses had been substituted; similar conditions applied in the case of a route for which tramway powers had been obtained but on which buses were being used. In another move to protect corporation interests the Commissioners ruled that, while Newcastle buses would be allowed to issue weekly season tickets, no other operator would be permitted to offer season tickets within the municipal boundaries, and such tickets for journeys outside could be issued only for a minimum period of one month. In effect, in exchange for a measure of protection, the municipal operators were being given no inducement to expand their field of influence, while the private operators (and their passengers) were being penalised on some short-distance urban traffic.

Not that there was necessarily an absence of co-operation between municipality and company; on the contrary, there were routes where the two regimes to all appearances worked happily together. The trunk routes between Newcastle and the coast were an obvious instance; we could travel on the buses of Newcastle Corporation or the Tyneside company, or those of United or Northern General or the nominally independent Wakefields Motors. Between South Shields and Cleadon, the buses of South Shields Corporation, Northern General and Sunderland District were in action on an agreed joint 7½min service, and tickets were inter-available. Of course in many cases the differences were more apparent than real; as we have seen, Northern General and Sunderland District were effectively one, while Northern also took over Wakefields in 1929 and the Tyneside company in 1936, among many other former independent operators which were acquired during the 1920s and 1930s by the bigger companies to make them bigger still.

Indeed in the face of this expansion there arose some anxiety that the Traffic Commissioners might attempt to adopt a policy of creating a monopoly on any individual route by issuing licences to only one operator. At a conference in Newcastle in 1931 representatives of interested local authorities went so far as to pass a resolution 'deprecating the creation of monopolies'; where there was more than one operator on a route, they urged, the licensing authority should continue to issue licences in proportion to each one's share of the service.

At the same time changes in the distribution of population were contributing to an alteration in the respective roles of company and municipal operations. New housing estates built during the 1920s and 1930s on the outskirts of towns and cities demanded new transport facilities, and since these estates were often constructed at the expense of the municipalities, naturally enough the municipal operators expected to provide these facilities. After all, it was argued, these people are our own citizens, whom we have been serving for so many years, and therefore we should retain this traffic. Not at all, said the companies; why should the municipalities push out their buses into areas traditionally ours? The companies, as a result of their own enterprise and at the risk of their own capital, had long been running buses on suburban and rural routes, many of which had been no more than marginally profitable. Now, as new houses sprang up to bring new passengers to the routes, the municipals wanted to claim this as their own exclusive territory, expand their boundaries and extend their routes. Certainly, countered the municipals; local services for local people should be run by local authorities, as they had traditionally been run. If we accept the companies' contention, they said, then we should be left with a shrinking central area with a diminishing population, while the companies would be thriving on our expanding suburbs. The outcome of the two differing viewpoints was often a difference of opinion which could only be resolved by compromise, perhaps reached after appeal to the Traffic Commissioners or the Ministry of Transport.

Sunderland faced the problem in an acute form, according to transport manager Charles Hopkins, who was outspoken about the role of his municipal undertaking. 'I have long held the opinion that local services should be for local authorities', he stated in 1939 at the end of a decade in which his vehicles had had to establish a form of coexistence with the companies. In 1930 Sunderland Corporation, in addition to its 80 tramcars, had only a dozen buses carrying fewer than three million passengers in the year; by 1939 the number had risen to 40, carrying nearly 12 million, but apparently the expansion had not gone as smoothly as it might have done. 'When I went to Sunderland in 1929', said Hopkins, 'the corporation were not turning a bus wheel'; to this tardiness on the part of the corporation to enter the bus business he attributed the strong foothold which the companies had been able to attain within the borough and the difficulties of the corporation in extending beyond its boundaries. Back in 1929, he recalled, in order to serve the North Hylton estate it had been necessary to agree that Northern General should provide half the service, and a similar agreement had been reached on the Castletown route. Hopkins complained that the companies had opposed the corporation's applications for new routes and had also sought the removal of the protection given to the corporation's tramcars by higher bus fares. In 1939 extension of the tramway was proposed in order to serve two large estates at Humbledon; he claimed that the inhabitants of the new houses were former customers of the trams in the older parts of the town, and should therefore be retained by the corporation. However, the companies contested the application and, according to Hopkins, said that if the corporation did extend its tracks they would apply to run their buses in parallel at the same fares as the tramcars.

Above:
While Sunderland Corporation's early postwar fleet comprised mainly Guys and Daimlers, it also included half-a-dozen 1947 AEC Regent III with 56-seat Roe bodies, such as No 85 here. No 85 was withdrawn in 1960. *AEC*

Below:
Bodywork by Newcastle-based Northern Coachbuilders was naturally to be found on many vehicles in the Tyne & Wear area, and typical of the maker's postwar double-deck design which appeared in 1946 was on Northern General AEC Regent No 985. *Ian Allan Library*

Below:
Northern General and Sunderland District routes were 'completely mixed up', with most worked jointly. As if to emphasise the point, buses of the two operators are seen here in succession in the same bay at Newcastle's Worswick Street bus station in the early 1950s. Northern General No 1576, a Leyland Tiger Cub with Weymann body, is on the service to Easington Lane, the original Sunderland District terminus; and Sunderland District No 243, a Brush-bodied Leyland Royal Tiger, is bound for Houghton-le-Spring and Durham. *G. H. F. Atkins*

South Shields had encountered a similar quandary; companies had opposed the corporation's extensions, including the introduction of trolleybuses on new routes into such areas as the developing Cleadon estate. Equally the corporation was convinced that it owed a duty to its citizens. 'Whilst one can be thankful that the companies, when introducing inter-town services, have conferred a certain amount of benefit internally', said Councillor R. H. Noble, chairman of the South Shields transport committee, 'I maintain that it is the privilege of a municipal transport committee to carry its own people.' The townsfolk regarded the local transport as their own and had asked for – and been given – services which probably for many years did not pay their way; they could not make the same demands of a private company. Now the municipalities had to accept a special responsibility: with slum clearance programmes leading to the removal of many people to new suburban homes, the corporation had a duty to provide the necessary transport services. Nevertheless the South Shields Corporation fleet remained only modest in size; the dozen buses carrying just on 1½ million passengers in 1930 had only increased to about 16 by the end of the decade, although the number of passengers almost doubled, but of course by this time the trolleybus was also playing a significant part in the town's transport network.

The new pattern of interwar housing had brought its own transport problems. The spaciousness afforded by the new standard of only 12 houses to the acre added to the quality of life for the residents but spelled trouble for the transport operator. Lines of communication between town centre and suburb were lengthened, fewer potential passengers were within the catchment area of the route, and off-peak traffic to a thinly-populated suburb could be less than the economic level. In the Tyne & Wear area the position was made worse during this period by the high level of unemployment; the peak-hour flows to and from work were reduced as fewer people had work to go to, while pleasure travel was beyond the budget of the unemployed man and his family.

During the 1930s Sunderland's Charles Hopkins was stressing the essential conditions for economic services: 'a greater density of population per acre, with the man of the house employed.' He quoted the case of his own town, where an estate of 350 houses with a 10min bus service provided a flow of not much more than seven passengers on each journey. 'A large estate is needed to be a reasonably good customer to any sort of transport service, and unless there is a fairly good return to be picked up between the suburb and the town, this service stands a poor chance of being a paying proposition.' He could have pointed to the corporation's Ford Hall estate extending over more than 130 acres where only about 1,000 houses had been built in the five years from 1928 to 1932. As to the effect of local unemployment, this had brought a 'heart-breaking' decline in traffic.

Retaining the population in the older areas was no less crucial. With extensive slum clearance programmes under way, the cleared areas could have become deserts in the heart of the town, with consequent damaging effects on established transport patterns. Moreover, the dispersion of population away from the docks and shipyards brought the additional burden of higher fares to those whose livelihood depended on the traditional industries. The case was forcefully put by the South Shields borough engineer, J. Paton Watson; while the suburban ideal of only 12 houses to the acre was justified at a time of industrial prosperity and high wages, it could not be realised in an area such as Tyneside in a period of industrial depression with low wages and much casual employment. By the start of the 1930s the corporation was going for the construction of blocks of flats in the older districts such as Tyne Dock where the density of dwellings could be as high as 20 to the acre, while 'cottage-type' dwellings were put up at a density of 14 or 15 to the acre. The transport department might well have heaved a sigh of relief.

As to the vehicles themselves, novelty was not lacking in some of the designs put on to the road by both company and municipality during this decade. In 1933 Sunderland District introduced AEC Regents with Brush-built bodies incorporating a front entrance and the stairway on the near side just ahead of the entrance, so that passengers for the upper deck had to turn sharp left immediately on boarding. The top deck seating included a front seat for four, and total seating was for 28 on the upper deck and 24 on the lower. A sliding door was fitted to the entrance. Later practice again favoured rear-entrance design, however, and conversions took place.

The central entrance layout was favoured by Sunderland Corporation for both tramcars and buses. Among the latter, the second half of the decade saw the multiplication of the design, incorporating a dual stairway which, although it reduced the total seating capacity, made for quicker loading and unloading. Among such vehicles were a number of Roe-bodied Daimlers, while an unusual note was struck by the appearance of a full-fronted design, mounted on a Crossley chassis provided with a special drop frame to accommodate the central-entrance English Electric body, which sported a streamlined finish in accord with that adopted for the contemporary tramcars. With its shapely 'flashes' and curved windscreen across the full front, it was of striking appearance. Seating capacity totalled 48, of which 23 were on the lower deck and 25 on the upper.

In single-deckers, the crown for innovation was surely earned by Northern General when the first of its own revolutionary side-engined vehicles made its debut in 1933. Very long and very low was the initial impression of these remarkable buses at a time when

Above:
A summer afternoon in Newcastle, so what better than a ride on an open-top bus? Newcastle Corporation No 233, a Daimler COG5 of 1939, had had its Northern Coachbuilders body converted to open top, and was later to go to the Llandudno & Colwyn Bay Electric Railway where it served as that company's No 2 from 1956 to 1961. *C. Carter*

Below:
The 'new look' front on the Newcastle Corporation bus of the mid-1950s; one of an order for 20, No 148 was an AEC Regent V with 62-seat Park Royal body. *Ian Allan Library*

Below right:
South Shields Corporation No 139, a Daimler CSG6 with 63-seat Roe body, was one of a batch delivered in 1962–63. By this time the corporation's 50 buses were carrying 15 million passengers a year against 18 million on the 50 trolleybuses they were soon to displace. *Ian Allan Library*

their stylish full front broke with the accepted half-cab tradition. In more recent times we have been forced to accept that the engine should go under the floor or at the back or at the side, indeed anywhere but at the old conventional front position; so it requires something of an effort of mind to conjure up the first shock of such a transposition as long ago as the early 1930s. Again we have become so used to the high-capacity vehicle that we have to think ourselves back to the disturbing occurrence of a single-decker with seats for as many as 45 passengers at a time when any self-respecting single-decker thought it was doing well with 32, and when many double-deckers could boast of no more than 48. But Northern General, serving an area criss-crossed by railways built long before high double-deck buses were envisaged, was plagued by low bridges which ensured that the bulk of its fleet was of the single-deck kind. In the interests of economical working as traffic increased on many such impeded routes, it wanted a single-decker which would carry a load comparable with that of a double-decker.

The result of its deliberations was this newcomer of 1933. The engine was mounted outside the frame on the offside of the three-axle chassis, on which was mounted the specially-designed 30ft long full-fronted forward-entrance body built by Short Brothers. On this first model the entrance was just behind the front wheels, but later versions had a longer front overhang with the entrance ahead of the wheels. So successful was the design that it soon became the hallmark of Northern General; up to 1939 a total of almost 70 appeared, some on six wheels (the SE6-type) and others on four wheels (SE4), some with luxuriously appointed coach bodies and others going to the associated Tynemouth company. In their later years some peculiar things happened (a six-wheeler was converted to a four-wheeler, and some vehicles found themselves being fitted with engines salvaged from war-surplus army tanks) but many continued to serve virtually unaltered in appearance until well into the postwar era, when the new-style single-deckers showed how far in advance of their time these veterans really were.

Meanwhile the bus had been working its own social revolution, bringing greater mobility to a population seeking lesser dependence on employment in the declining traditional industries. Significant of the new age was the growth of employment opportunities in such locations as the Team Valley trading estate, established in 1936, where transport was essentially based on road services. The trend became even more marked in the post-1945 development period. The swing to road was symbolised by Northern General's experience; when the LNER had bought its interest in the company in 1929 there had been some 80 passenger railway stations within its area, but by the early 1960s this number had been practically halved, and further rail withdrawals were soon to reduce it still more.

11 Modern Tramcars and Trolleybuses

In general these Newcastle trolleybuses represent the best that have so far been produced in this country, and for comfort and smooth riding they have made a pleasant impression on the people of Tyneside.
Transport World, 1935

Even at first glance we could see that Sunderland Corporation tramcar No 86 was something special. The colour scheme, for one thing, featured a 'streamlined' effect at the ends, rather reminiscent of the prow of a speed boat, while the sides were flush panelled and the ends neatly enclosed. Internally there were more surprises; on the lower deck, transverse seats were upholstered in blue moquette, while – even more remarkable – on the upper deck the seats were upholstered in red hide instead of displaying the traditional polished wood. The vestibule was arranged with a central pole and rail to separate passengers for the upper deck from those wishing to enter the lower saloon. The EMB hornless truck of 8ft 6in wheelbase with two 50hp motors gave speedy acceleration and a smooth ride, and the car glided to a halt with the aid of air-operated brakes. With a total seating capacity of 62 and an overall length of just over 30ft, the car weighed in at 13 tons. This was No 86 in 1932, when it was produced by the Transport Department as a prototype for future designs. As a result, a dozen similar cars followed in 1933, and even more revolutionary models were in the offing.

By this time tramways were already falling under the advance of the motorbus. In the Tyne & Wear areas the Sunderland District system had closed in 1925, Jarrow in 1929, Tyneside in 1930 and Tynemouth in 1931. Newcastle Corporation had accepted that the recently completed link across the new Tyne Bridge had been the final extension to the city's tramways. Yet here on Wearside, Sunderland Corporation was apparently sailing against the wind in embarking on a period of tramway modernisation. Following agreement on transport manager Charles Hopkins' 1929 recommendation that the town's tramways should be retained, improvement had been going ahead noticeably; within three years, some £130,000 had been spent, and by 1934 this had risen to more than £200,000. The work included track reconstruction, alteration to the overhead to allow the use of bow collectors instead of trolley poles (Sunderland was the first undertaking in Britain to complete the change), and new cars such as No 86.

The case for the tramways, as expounded by Hopkins, was based on their suitability to the town's transport needs, and the high cost of dispensing with them rather than retaining them. Hopkins pointed out that the tramways served the main traffic arteries and ran to and through the town centre. Every route was densely built-up and generally required at least a 5min service. The cars were better able to cope with the peak periods (including the midday rush) and to deal with surges of traffic following the onset of bad weather – an outbreak of rain at Seaburn on a Bank Holiday was an obvious case in point. They could better handle the extra burdens of seaside trippers on a fine summer day, or the football crowds to Roker Park. The 62-seat tramcars had the edge in capacity over the buses, which were generally no more than 48-seaters – and moreover the Road Traffic Act had now limited the standing load to only five. It was just not economical to attempt to meet all traffic requirements with motorbuses, especially at the low fares which were charged in Sunderland where we could ride 1½ miles for 1d or more than three miles for 2d.

Replacement of the tramcars by either motorbuses or trolleybuses would also have proved a costly process. Hopkins put the total cost of conversion to buses at almost £280,000, while a change to trolleybuses would have entailed an expenditure of nearly £300,000. The main item was of course the rolling stock, at a cost of £225,000, but in addition £25,000 would have had to be spent on a garage (since the existing tram depots were unsuitable for non-railed vehicles) and some £27,000 for removing the redundant tracks in the streets. For trolleybuses, an extra item was some £27,000 for the conversion of the overhead. Also to be borne in mind was the shorter life of either bus or trolleybus – only eight to 12 years.

By contrast, expenditure on tramway improvements in the five years following Hopkins' 1929 report amounted to £200,000. Of this total, track reconstruction (including new rails and welded joints) accounted for well over half, at £114,000, and in a period of high unemployment this task had provided useful work for local men. New underground feeder cables, with about 100% greater capacity, had cost some £32,000 (significantly, when the new feeders were installed, negative cables had been included suitable for trolleybus operation if it should be decided to make a change at some future time). Adapting the overhead for the use of bow collectors had cost only about £5,000;

much of the existing equipment had been retained, while the extra standards required had been bought cheaply from other undertakings where they had been made redundant. With the whole system thus brought up to a high standard, the cost of maintenance in coming years would be minimised. On rolling stock, expenditure had amounted to more than £50,000, but Hopkins was in no doubt of the popularity of his modern tramcars. 'The rapid acceleration and speed of the modern car, with upholstered seating, and well-sprung truck riding on a jointless track', he wrote, 'have definitely captivated the imagination of the travelling public.'

Greater safety was also claimed for the tramcars, a factor which, as Hopkins conceded, was not solely a matter for the transport operator but was an important consideration in the light of local conditions. 'Sunderland, especially at weekends,' he pointed out, 'is the rendezvous of the people from the surrounding townships or the thickly-populated County of Durham, the result being that the pavements in the town are so hopelessly crowded that people overflow on to the fairway between the kerbstone and car lines, which for practical purposes becomes another crowded footpath'. Under such conditions the 'mobility' of the bus or trolleybus would be a 'definite menace', since the rate of accidents would counteract any advantage that might be derived from kerbside loading. It was perhaps ironical that some 20 years later, when motor traffic had so greatly increased, the overcrowded conditions in Fawcett Street (the town's main thoroughfare) served to hasten the demise of the tramcars.

Reorganisation, including a reduction in administrative expenses and an increase in scheduled speeds, resulted in a substantial decrease in operating costs. Hopkins produced figures showing that total operating cost per car mile had fallen from well over 14d in 1929 to only 10.5d in 1934, while the ratio of working expenses to traffic revenue had dropped from over 82% to some 67%. As a result, the net profit had gone up from only £10,000 in 1929 to well over £32,000 in 1934. This was no mean achievement at a time when receipts were being drastically curtailed by the continuing trade depression, when unemployment was at an exceptionally high level and workmen's traffic severely restricted. Receipts per car mile dropped from 18d in 1929 to less than 16d in 1934. If conditions had been more prosperous, there is little doubt that the transport department's position would have been more profitable, for as some recovery set in during the later 1930s, net profit amounted to £29,000 in 1936 and about £40,000 in 1937. By 1939, with the easing of the worst of the depression, the cars were carrying more passengers: over 36 million in the year, against fewer than 30 million in 1934. Revenue per car mile had also risen to over 16d, but at the same time operating expenses per mile had gone up to over 12d and the ratio of operating expenses to receipts had risen to some 77%, so that the resultant net profit came down to about £21,000. If there were signs of further problems ahead, Hopkins' policy served to secure the survival of Sunderland's tramways into the 1950s, by which time rapidly rising costs, coupled with increased traffic congestion and the need for new routes, brought them to the end of the line.

During the years of the 1930s, however, modernisation was proceeding on cars and equipment, producing some interesting innovations in a form of transit widely regarded as obsolescent. Pantographs replaced the bow collectors, which had suffered from coastal gales blowing them off contact with the wires; a new extension was opened to the seafront; and at Seaburn a turning circle was constructed to speed the turnround of cars carrying holiday crowds. And the new cars continued to arrive, the most original of them comprising a series of central-entrance streamliners. The first, No 99, was put into service in 1934 and was an impressive bogie car more than 38ft long and with seats for 76 passengers. With a centre entrance fitted with folding doors, curved roof windows and smart styling and livery, it attracted a good deal of attention; not the least obvious characteristics were the twin headlamps, in place of the traditional single central headlamp, a touch of inspiration in making a psychological break with the old-fashioned image of the tramcar. However, lengthy No 99 proved to be a little excessive for the fierce curves and limited clearances of the town's tracks, so further cars of the same general design built from 1935 to 1940 were shorter versions on four wheels; to design a central-entrance car on a single truck required no little ingenuity in insetting the framework to allow for the entrance, and the result was a small fleet of outstanding vehicles that added a touch of distinction to a supposedly outmoded genus.

Both Newcastle and South Shields meanwhile had opted for the trolleybus. Newcastle Corporation's first route, inaugurated on 1 October 1935, was on quite an extensive scale, running west to east across the city for almost 10 miles and calling for a fleet of 30 vehicles. Westward it extended well beyond the former tram terminus at Fox & Hounds in Westgate Road to penetrate a growing bus-served residential area to reach Denton Burn, where a lengthy loop was provided. Passing through the city, where a loop in St Nicholas Street offered a central terminal point, it journeyed eastward through Byker and Walker to Wallsend. Traffic on the line was mixed in character, varying from the suburban residences in the west to the shipyards and engineering works in the east, while added complexity was given by the midday peak.

The new fleet consisted of six-wheel 60-seat double-deckers, again with the front exit that was established practice on the tramcars, but this time with power-operated doors. The first batch comprised an interesting mixture, as seemed to be a not uncommon practice when operators wanted to discover which

Sunderland's tramways.

Above:
'Each route is heavily populated and receives a minimum service of 5 minutes', transport manager Charles Hopkins stated in his report proposing tramway modernisation. Safety in working services through the town's none-too-wide main thoroughfare Fawcett Street was a factor in favour of retaining the tramcars, although increasing road traffic eventually created a serious bottleneck. Photographed in 1950, No 30 (one of a batch of 1931–32 English Electric cars purchased from Huddersfield) loads at the queue barrier on service to Grangetown. *C. Carter*

Above right:
Although the proposed connection to South Shields was never constructed, the extension along Dykelands Road was opened in 1937 to provide a useful additional route to the sea at Seaburn. The excellent state of the track and the road surface, and the neatly strung overhead for pantograph operation, are worthy of note. *R. Brook*

Right:
The apogee of tramcar design in Tyne & Wear. One of Sunderland's central-entrance streamliners of 1935–40 (left) passes South Shields' sole example of a similar type, built in 1936 and later purchased by Sunderland, a reminder of what might have been if the two separate systems had been connected. *R. Brook*

SHOP AT
BINNS
DURHAM RD

SHOP AT
BINNS
CIRCLE
CIRCLE
WOODS
SHOP AT
BINNS

RESERVED
4
BVK 806
BVK 590

WALKER
4A
BUS
STOP
BVK 803

The dawn of Newcastle's trolleybus era.

Left:
Employed on driver training before the start of service in 1935, No 16 (an AEC 664T with 60-seat Brush body) traverses West Road on the Denton Burn route. Note the use of side bracket arms instead of span wires. This suburban thoroughfare on the western outskirts of the city was beyond the tram terminus on the main road to Carlisle; the amount and character of the traffic is interesting, with commercial vehicles, buses and private cars all in evidence.
Ian Allan Library

Below left:
In action: in a different setting on the Wallsend route, No 13 was also an AEC 664T but with English Electric body. Tram tracks are still visible in the sett-paved street. *Ian Allan Library*

Above:
A batch of Guy BTX with Metropolitan-Cammell bodies delivered to Newcastle in 1937.
Ian Allan Library

Below:
Still in its pristine state before delivery to Newcastle in 1935 is this as yet unnumbered Guy. The arrangement of the forward exit with electrically-operated door is apparent. *Ian Allan Library*

marque best served their needs. Of the chassis, 10 each came from AEC, Guy and Karrier, while 20 of the bodies were supplied by Metropolitan-Cammell-Weymann, and five each by English Electric and Brush, all painted in a new colour scheme of yellow with brown waist line. Existing tramway overhead was converted along about seven miles of the route, but the remainder required entirely new equipment.

Results immediately appeared to justify the changeover. In the first full year of operation, when some 16 million passengers were carried, the new trolleybuses returned a net profit of over £35,000; average revenue per vehicle mile was more than 19d while operating expenses were just 11d. By contrast, the tramcars were bringing in only 16d per car mile, while their operating expenses amounted to almost 13d. Against such an encouraging background, further conversions and extensions followed, until before the end of 1938 a fleet of a hundred trolleybuses was working over some 22 miles of routes.

The genesis of the change could be traced back several years before the move was made. As early as 1930 the Transport Committee recommended to the City Council that no further extensions should be made to the tramways, and that 'other forms of transport' should be adopted 'when and where desirable to meet the growing needs of the city'. While it did not advocate the general abolition of the tramways, it proposed 'in every case where the tramway becomes worn out and must be renewed, to give careful consideration to the question whether the route can be more efficiently served by a form of transport other than tramcars.' In any such consideration, attention would be paid to the convenience of, and the cost to, the travelling public. The Committee believed that such a policy was preferable to a complete and immediate replacement of the tramcars, which on most routes were still 'the best and most economical form of transport'. But the great obstacle to continued tramway operation was highlighted by the fact that whereas before 1914 the cost of permanent way renewal had amounted to about £10,000 for each mile of double track, during the 1920s the cost had more than doubled to £22,000 per mile.

Nevertheless there was still some uncertainty about pursuing any too drastic transformation. In the new year of 1931, after protracted consideration of a report by the general manager, the Transport Committee found itself faced with two alternative courses of action. Should the tramways be abolished entirely? This extreme was not actively advocated except by a few who deplored spending further money on a mode of transport which they regarded as obsolescent; the majority were reluctant to dispose of assets representing substantial investments. Or should the tramways be improved, by the provision of better and faster cars able to offer a better service within the city, while the motorbus should be used in the outer areas where it would prove a more economical vehicle? It was not an easy decision to make, and the Committee can be excused if, after giving it much deliberation, it postponed the fateful day.

But circumstances continued to close in. Along came the manager with a special report in which he stressed that the undertaking needed extra revenue of some £25,000 a year for at least four years if the tramways were to be put on to a sound financial basis; and to get this amount of money, fares would have to be raised. Then there were complaints about the state of the tracks, particularly in Osborne Road and Westgate Road. How much, the Committee asked, would it cost to put matters right? Again the figure of £20,000 a mile for track renewal loomed large, so perhaps replacement by another form of transport would be preferable? During the course of this year some members of the Committee, including its chairman Alderman Mayne, had visited a number of other towns to have a look at their trolleybuses, with which they were reported to be 'greatly impressed'. Nevertheless a decision was still postponed, and it was not until towards the end of the year that the Committee made up its mind that in view of the high cost of track renewal the tramway in Osborne Road should be replaced by motor buses.

However, when the City Council looked at the idea in the early weeks of 1932, it did not approve. Instead it decreed that the tramcars should continue, and that the Committee should get on with the job of renewing the tracks. Such a task of course called for money, and this proved not to be forthcoming, for by the spring the Council had had further thoughts and had now made up its mind that the estimated expenditure of £13,599 should not be made at this time (somehow the original estimate of £20,000 a mile appears to have shrunk over the months); instead, it agreed to spend the much more modest sum of £2,000 in order to undertake temporary repairs which would be sufficient to allow the cars to run over the tracks for another two or three years. In the event they continued to run until 1938, when trolleybuses at last replaced them.

That obstinate figure of £20,000 a mile again reared its head in 1933, when it was again stressed that this was the amount that would have to be spent if the tramcars were to be kept going along certain sections of track. A special sub-committee now went into the matter and examined the possibility of substituting other modes of transport. Subsequently the Corporation obtained powers in 1934 to operate trolleybuses in replacement of tramcars on the Westgate Road and Wallsend routes, while general trolleybus powers were obtained in the following year. The cost of the whole installation of the first trolleybus route was put at some £70,000, whereas retention of the tramway would have involved an expenditure of £90,000 for the purposes of track renewal alone. Work on the conversion was underway in the spring of 1935, with the first trial runs during the summer. Some economy in the cost of the work was attributable to the foresight of the

Above:
South Shields began to run its first trolleybuses in 1936 and one of the initial vehicles was No 203, a Karrier E4 with 56-seat Weymann body, seen here shortly after service started on King George Road. After air raid damage, No 203 returned with a new utility body from Weymann in 1942. *Ian Allan Library*

Below:
New in South Shields in 1948 was this Karrier W4 with Northern Coachbuilders body, photographed on service 11 to Marsden Grotto. Although the system was re-equipped in the postwar years, abandonment was proposed in 1959 and the last trolleybus ran on 29 April 1964.

Above:
Posed for the camera before taking up its duties is Gateshead & District No 10, one of the Park Royal-bodied Guy Arabs introduced in 1950 for tram replacement. It still carries the legal name Gateshead & District *Tramways* Company before this was changed in line with the changed mode of operation. Buses took over the Heworth and Wrekenton routes on 5 March 1950. *Ian Allan Library*

Left:
Summer sunshine in suburban Gateshead; Gateshead & District Tramways No 32 (one of the rebuilt 1901 series) waits at the Saltwell Park terminus. The possibility of replacement by trolleybuses was still in the air. *G. S. Hearse*

electric tramway planners of the turn of the century; they had laid down spare underground cable conduits along all their routes, and some of these were now employed to carry additional feeders for the trolleybuses. A factor urged in favour of the electric vehicle rather than the motorbus – in Newcastle as well as in South Shields – was that it used electricity generated from home-produced coal, a point which had an obvious appeal in an area based on this major industry.

South Shields came on to the trolleybus scene just a year after Newcastle, when its first route was inaugurated on 12 October 1936 between the Market Place and suburban Prince Edward Road, a distance of about three miles. Powers had been obtained to operate trolleybuses instead of tramcars on all routes, as well as on routes beyond the existing tracks, and the new service represented the first initial step in this direction; although it paralleled the tramway for part of its length, it was not in fact a direct replacement. Again the cost of tramway extension ruled it out of the realms of practicality; the area served was still under development, and was clearly in need of new transport facilities to meet the needs of the growing numbers of inhabitants of the new suburban dwellings. The Cleadon Light Railway, constructed only a decade earlier, still looked a possible candidate for extension, and there was no immediate suggestion that this sleeper-track along Ridgeway should be withdrawn, although it was now paralleled for part of its length by the new trolley vehicles. However, the town's new transport manager, E. R. L. Fitzpayne, pointed out that if the tramway was to serve the desired purpose, it would need to be projected to Marsden, and the total cost of such a scheme would amount to £55,000; in the existing financial situation he could not recommend such a course. Instead the installation of the trolleybus route cost no more than £14,500. This sum included an order for four vehicles at a cost of some £8,400, and these appeared as four-wheel Karriers with Weymann double-deck bodies.

Although there was no formal opening ceremony, the Mayor of South Shields drove the first vehicle, and *Transport World* was able to report that its 'comfort and silence drew high praise from those present'. Considering the fact that there was no 'formal ceremony', the list of those present reads like a *Who's Who* of the area's transport notabilities: among them were, naturally enough, members of South Shields Council as well as the town's newly-appointed transport manager H. Muscroft and his immediate predecessor Fitzpayne, now translated to be deputy manager at Edinburgh; but also in attendance were Newcastle's redoubtable transport chairman Alderman Mayne and his general manager, plus the chairman of Sunderland's transport committee, the traffic superintendent from Bradford, the chairman of the Northern Area Traffic Commissioners, and the Newcastle district passenger manager of the LNER. Alderman Mayne was able to put in an encouraging word about the modern mode of transit; in the short time since his city had started to use it, receipts had gone up by 30% and were still rising, a happy augury for the new recruit.

But if any of his distinguished hearers nourished visions of the twin wires being strung up between South Shields and Newcastle or Sunderland, they were destined to be disappointed. While South Shields' trolleybuses reached out along the breezy coast road to Marsden, where they could have held out a welcoming hand to their counterparts from Sunderland if that town had ever been tempted to the trolley, and while they negotiated the tangle of railway tracks to circle round Tyne Dock, from where they could have advanced through Jarrow to join up with Gateshead's wires if that town's company had been converted, in reality South Shields and Newcastle were to remain the only two adherents to the trolleybus in Tyne & Wear.

Not that others had failed to look closely or to feel the impulse to convert; but, as with the tramways in a previous generation, problems reared their head to frustrate any grand design. The story of how the Gateshead company very nearly made the change is one of the classic might-have-beens. Statutory powers were obtained, a whole new fleet was on order, and Newcastle's trolleybuses even carried Gateshead destinations on their indicator blinds in anticipation of through running to their neighbour. After the long-delayed linking of the two undertakings across the Tyne bridges in the 1920s and the establishment of joint tramcar services, it seemed a not unreasonable expectation that conversion in Newcastle might be accompanied by a similar process in Gateshead to ensure the continuance of through working. Yet after a protracted period of negotiations, proposals and counter-proposals, no trolleybuses ever ran in Gateshead.

The basic stumbling block was that long-hallowed tradition of imperfect harmony between one authority and another which had from time to time bedevilled the integration of the transport pattern in parts of the Tyne and Wear region over the years. In this instance, Newcastle Corporation wanted to run its trolleybuses into Gateshead, while Gateshead Corporation desired to buy up the company in its midst and replace the tramcars by its own trolleybuses, and at the centre of the controversy the Gateshead & District Tramways Co put its faith in the motorbus as the most satisfactory type of vehicle to serve its routes. To aggravate the situation still further, the advent of World War 2 delayed any drastic action to resolve the matter, and the aftermath of the war posed problems in the supply of new vehicles, while added uncertainty in the postwar era was inspired by a government plan which would have resulted in the nationalisation of local transport undertakings. In the event, the Gateshead tramcars enjoyed a lengthy reprieve, and when they eventually retired in 1950–51 their successors were not trolleybuses but diesels.

A detailed account of the episode is given us by the historians of the Newcastle trolleybus, T. P. Canneaux and N. H. Hanson, so suffice it here to recall that Newcastle Corporation, anxious to maintain through operation, backed Gateshead Corporation's bid in 1937 to obtain powers to acquire the Gateshead company and install its own trolleybuses. As a result of this move the company, which had already proposed to substitute motorbuses, felt constrained to obtain its own trolleybus powers, which it did under its 1938 Act. In the course of its passage through Parliament the Bill had been opposed by Gateshead Corporation which had also had the support of Newcastle Corporation in the person of transport committee chairman Alderman Mayne. Giving evidence against the Bill in the House of Lords, Mayne stressed that his city's policy was to replace tramways by trolleybuses, and he foresaw that 'sooner or later' Newcastle and Gateshead would 'probably have to amalgamate'; when that came about, he stated, it would be 'unsatisfactory' if the corporation were serving one area of the community and the company another, a logical view which served to emphasise the need for an enlarged transport area, if not the aggrandisement of the city of Newcastle itself.

The outbreak of war in 1939 came before the new powers could be implemented, but then in 1946 it was announced that the Gateshead company had put in orders for a total of 83 trolleybuses at a cost of £250,000, to be used to replace the tramways within two years. The new vehicles were to be 56-seat double-deckers, a fact which would call for the raising of obstructive bridges which were too low to admit double-deck buses, let alone double-deck trolleys. The first routes to be converted were to be those to Heworth and Wrekenton, on which Newcastle cars were also engaged on the through services. However, further complications including the short supply of trolleybuses (which obliged Newcastle Corporation to turn to the motorbus for immediate replacements in order to clear tramcars from the accounts as soon as possible), the problems of the purchase of the Gateshead company by Gateshead Corporation and its position in the light of impending nationalisation, plus the continued belief by the company that buses were best, eventually resulted in the Gateshead & District Tramways Act of 1950 which enabled the company to reliquish its trolleybus powers and instead to operate motorbuses; in line with this move, it also changed its title to the Gateshead & District Omnibus Co. In due course therefore the last Gateshead tramcars ceased to run on 4 April 1951, by which time they were the last company-operated trams in England and the last tramway operations of the once mighty BET empire.

Newcastle Corporation meanwhile had itself relinquished its last tramcars on 4 March 1950, though ironically for more than another year the Gateshead company's cars were to continue running into the city. At the same time the trolley fleet was renewed with the influx of more than 180 vehicles between 1948 and 1950; of these, there were various permutations of Northern Coachbuilders and Metro-Cammell bodies, some 7ft 6in wide and others 8ft, on both four-wheel and six-wheel chassis by Sunbeam and BUT. Compared with prewar, a noticeable omission was the absence of the front exit. By the 1950s the trolleybus occupied a prominent position in the municipal fleet, its total strength of about 200 vehicles comparing with some 250 motorbuses. And new routes had also been brought into use: to Gosforth Park, South Gosforth, Benton and Heaton in 1948, to Grange Estate in 1950.

Nevertheless the trolleybus did not command unqualified admiration. Opinion from the City Engineer's department, who were after all charged with responsibility for ensuring the optimum efficiency of the streets, conceded that the trolleybus offered certain advantages over the motorbus, but held that from the point of view of traffic congestion there were 'grave objections' to its use. Basically it was route-bound, it could not stray from its wires, and so lacked manoeuvrability in busy traffic. One vehicle could not overtake another, while in general, it was claimed, its average speed compared unfavourably with that of the motorbus.

The 'buses or trolleybuses?' controversy boasts a venerable pedigree, for in Newcastle's case it can be traced back at least as early as 1912, when the city came near to obtaining its first trolley vehicles. At that time something of a 'trackless mania' was seething; Leeds and Bradford had both actually started to run trolleybuses in 1911, and many other places had been inspired to look around to see where this new mode of transit could fit into their own town. In Newcastle in 1910 there were thoughts that it could be installed to link outlying suburbs and villages to the tramway network: perhaps Heaton to Benton, or Scotswood to Newburn or Blaydon, or maybe along the Fenham Road to Westerhope? Committees and sub-committees pondered and reported, and subsequently powers for trolley vehicle operation were sought in the Corporation's Bill of 1911. But then things seemed to go awry, and in the event the Corporation emerged with an Act empowering it to operate motorbuses instead. As well as running within the city, these could also go to Westerhope and Walbottle, but because of objections from the Tyneside company another outside route, to Seaton Burn, was rejected. Without wasting much more time in cogitation, the Corporation went ahead and ordered the new vehicles from Tilling Stevens, becoming the first municipality to place an order for petrol-electric buses.

Why no trolleybuses? According to Councillor Rodgers – who was not only chairman of the Tramways Committee but chairman of the Corporation's Parliamentary Committee – the rock on which the trolley foundered was that of road maintenance. To obtain powers to operate outside the city boundaries, the Corporation would have been required to pay for road maintenance on the routes concerned, and on this point Councillor Rodgers 'declined to give any undertaking'. So the trolleybus powers came out of the Bill and the Corporation went for buses instead.

General manager Ernest Hatton had also declared in favour of the motorbus rather than the trolley. No doubt with thoughts of the recent Parliamentary proceedings in mind, he pointed to the problems involved in obtaining the necessary statutory powers, but he also advanced what was to become an increasingly strong argument in favour of the motor bus, namely its flexibility. It could be transferred from one route to another as traffic demands dictated without being confined by its wires. But another aspect of his argument recalls the prevailing contemporary view that the trolleybus could act as a temporary stopgap tramcar, employed only to open up a route which would later become a 'real' tramway as traffic developed; if motorbuses were used for this pioneering role, he claimed, they could be simply switched to other services if their route was thus replaced, whereas the trolleybus would become redundant.

Meanwhile the petrol-electrics were proclaimed by Councillor Rodgers as the best of both worlds: Newcastle had got electric buses, but without the high capital cost of overhead equipment. It had spent £850 on each bus, but it had saved well over £1,000 a mile by not having had to string up the overhead. The Corporation was well satisfied, he announced, and 'they would not fall back to the trackless trolley even if they could'. Though there may have been a hint of making a virtue of necessity, the Corporation nevertheless adhered to the motorbus for its wider territorial ambitions for the next 20 years.

Left:
Four-wheelers were in the minority in Newcastle's trolleybus fleet. The 1948–50 renewal programme included a number of Sunbeams with Northern Coachbuilders bodies, including No 550 seen here when new.

Below:
Buses or trolleybuses? A Newcastle Leyland Titan overtakes one of the 1948–50 Metropolitan-Cammell bodied BUTs. Although the trolleybus formed a large part of the Corporation's transport operations and possessed the merits of silent running and utilising home-produced electricity, it was criticised for lack of mobility in congested streets. The last Newcastle services ceased on 1 October 1966, so ending trolleybus operation in Tyne & Wear.

12 Electrics in Action

The system of electrification which the North Eastern Railway has inaugurated on Tyneside has been brought to a fine state of perfection . . . The vehicles themselves are a great improvement on the ordinary coach, being a sort of glorified electric tramcar, and the patronage is an eloquent testimony to their popularity.

The Railway Magazine, 1908

The long awaited electrification of the Newcastle–South Shields railway eventually became a reality in 1938, when a regular service of electric trains started on 14 March of that year. While the basic frequency remained at the 20 minutes of steam days when about five million passengers a year were being carried, the throughout journey time for the 11 miles with its seven intermediate stops was reduced from 33 or 34 minutes to 27 minutes. Peak hour reliefs were also run between Gateshead East and South Shields, avoiding the use of the busy tracks over the High Level bridge. Modernised 1920 stock was employed, and in order that eight-car trains could be accommodated, platforms were lengthened at the intermediate stations of Hebburn, Jarrow, Tyne Dock and High Shields.

Replacement of steam traction on the South Shields line materially eased the operating situation at Newcastle Central. Trains using the High Level bridge and the famous crossings were no longer confined to the one platform where a spur was available to hold the necessary turnover locomotive, while the elimination of the associated light engine movements to and from Gateshead sheds helped to alleviate the congestion on the tracks across the bridge.

Consideration had been given to the possible use of diesel trains on the South Shields line, perhaps based on the LNER's experience with diesel cars built by Armstrong-Whitworth. In 1931 this firm had supplied a diesel-electric car, fitted for working in multiple unit or with control trailers, and this carried out some impressive tests in the Newcastle area. It went up the steeply graded line from Newcastle to Blackhill in a running time of only 34 minutes against the 41 minutes of the steam trains; then going on to Durham, it reached speeds of over 60mph on the main line back to Newcastle. While such cars bearing names like *Tyneside Venturer*, *Lady Hamilton* and *Northumbrian* were to be seen in operation, electrification was decided on for the South Shields line because the conversion could economically be carried out as an extension of the existing system and could be included as part of the general modernisation plan.

Carried out between 1933 and 1938, the modernisation programme aimed at an all-round improvement of the electric services, not only by the provision of new rolling stock, but also by other installations and works designed to expedite operations. The new station at West Monkseaton, a neat two-platform affair with modern style buildings on an overbridge, was opened in 1933. Platforms were lengthened at Walker Gate, Howdon and Percy Main to take eight-car trains, and North Shields tunnel, originally too narrow to permit two trains to pass on the curve, was widened. For several days during 1936 steam trains took over from electrics while some 500 men were engaged in repositioning the conductor rail by some 3in in accordance with the latest Ministry of Transport standards, while the necessary alterations to the car collector shoes were being made in Gosforth sheds. Meanwhile, from 1934 heavier section conductor rails had been gradually installed to reduce voltage drop. At the end of 1937 reversible working was introduced on two of the four tracks between Central and Manors, the busiest section of the LNER's northeast area, in order to allow greater flexibility in operations.

On 30 July 1937 the Lord Mayor of Newcastle officially launched into service the first of the new trains. This reintroduced the old bright colour scheme of red and cream, a happy sight to many after years of the LNER teak brown which had displaced the NER's colours. The new cars were of all-steel construction, with large windows and sliding doors. In accordance with favoured LNER practice, the cars were arranged as two-car articulated units, an interesting anticipation of today's articulated Metrocar units. Internally the old type of reversible seats had been banished and instead there were deep and comfortable bucket seats upholstered in moquette.

In all, 64 of the twin sets arrived from the Metropolitan–Cammell Carriage & Wagon Co, with electrical equipment supplied by Associated Manufacturers of Electric Traction Equipment, one of whose members was British Thomson-Houston, suppliers of equipment on the original NER stock. In line with the tradition established by their predecessors, the new trains were not all of the same kind; again there had to be various permutations of first and third class, and of cars with and without luggage compartments. Some of the units consisted of motor third with luggage compartment plus a trailer first, while others comprised a motor third with no luggage plus a trailer third; others again had no driving compartment at the trailer end and so could not run singly. It all added up to flexibility in train formation to meet varying demands.

With the introduction of the new trains, the scheduled time for the out-and-back was reduced: an all-stations now took only 53 minutes compared with

Electric trains at Pelaw on the Newcastle–South Shields service.

Above:
A train of articulated twins departs for South Shields.

Below:
Bound for Newcastle, a set of the refurbished 1920 stock looks as though it has seen strenuous duty. The leading car is a motor luggage composite; the single line destination indicator is augmented by a 'Stopping' board in the front window. Electric trains on the South Shields line were withdrawn on 6 January 1963.
W. Hubert Foster

Electric operations at Newcastle Central in the later days of the LNER, with trains of the Metropolitan-Cammell twin sets introduced in 1937.

Above:
A six-car train from South Shields leaves the High Level bridge and negotiates the crossovers to enter the station. *Ian Allan Library*

Below:
Two north side trains await departure: on the left an empty to South Gosforth depot and on the right a stopping train to the coast. *W. Hubert Foster*

The extensive modernisation of the Tyneside electric lines carried out during the 1930s included both new and refurbished rolling stock.

Top:
Driving trailer third of NER pattern as refurbished for the South Shields service; it is in the 1941 blue and white livery with the LNER totem.
Crown copyright, National Railway Museum, York

Above:
Two of the 1937 two-car articulated sets when new, in the red and white livery. The leading unit is all third, while the other has first-class accommodation in the trailer car.
Crown copyright, National Railway Museum, York

Left:
This view of the saloon in a third-class car of the 1937 twin units shows the bucket-type seating.
Real Photographs

At South Gosforth car sheds in 1947.

Above:
Emerging from the depot are two-car articulated units of the 1937 type stock for the north side services. The destination indicators show 'Newcastle Stopping'.
G. S. Hearse

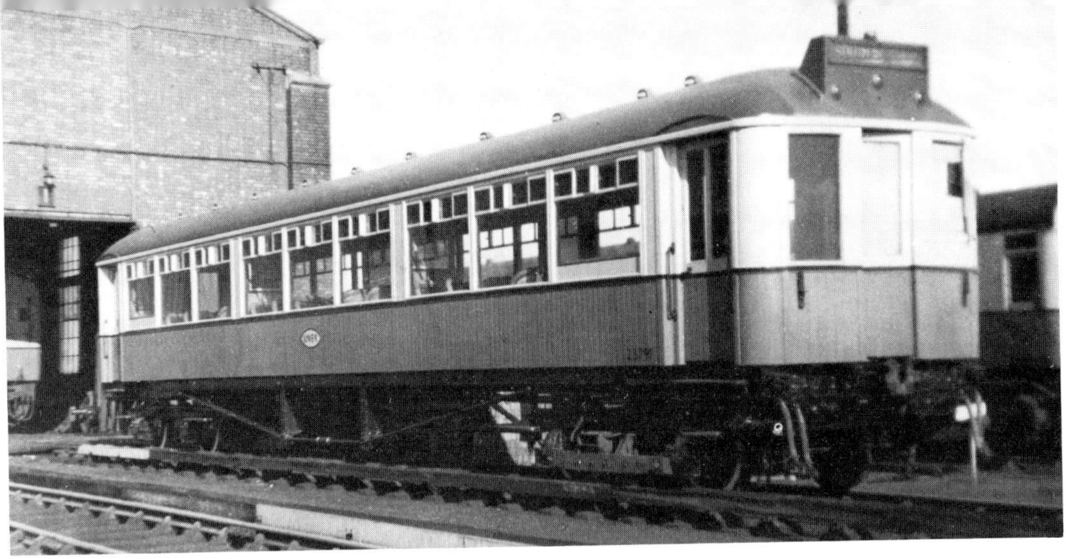

Above:
Apparently recently come from the paint shop is one of the NER 1922 motor cars as rebuilt in 1938 for the South Shields service; it still retains its matchboarded sides, bucket seats, and single line indicators with three lamps. *G. S. Hearse*

Below:
A six-car train for the coast pulls out of Manors East on the four-track electrified section between Manors and Heaton Junction. The overhead wires of the Quayside branch are just visible on the extreme left. *Ian Allan Library*

the original 63 minutes for the 20-mile circuit. From Central, Tynemouth was reached in 20 minutes via the direct coast line, and Whitley Bay in 25 minutes either by this way or round the top of the circle via Benton.

The timetable for the north side lines under the availability of the new trains reflected not only the desire to meet bus competition, but also the developing coastal residential area as well as the beginnings of recovery from the long trade depression. Normal weekday service provided eight trains every hour between Newcastle and the coast; a 20min service operated via the north side of the circle and a 20min service on the south side, all of which were stopping trains. An hourly frequency continued on the Riverside line between Central and Tynemouth. Another hourly service was the 'express' between Newcastle and the coast, generally via Benton. Additional expresses were put on during peak hours; between 5pm and 6pm, for example, three expresses traversed the Benton route and a further two ran via Wallsend. These combined with the ordinary stopping service to provide in the outward direction during this one rush hour a total seating capacity of around 4,500; allowing for standing room, total capacity was about 8,000 passengers.

A midday peak was also catered for, because the frequent service and relatively short journey time encouraged many city workers to travel to and from their seaside homes at the lunch break; between noon and 1pm about a dozen departures pulled out of Central, with a corresponding number of arrivals between about 1.15 and 2.15. Workmen's extras added to the flow; these particularly served stations near to the shipyards, notably Walker, Wallsend and Willington Quay, on which workers converged from both directions.

Summer peaks, when crowds flocked to the seaside on a fine Sunday or bank holiday, raised further operating problems. While in winter a half-hourly service would suffice, in summer this might have to be substantially augmented. During the 1930s the holiday months of June, July and August saw an average total of as many as 30,000 tickets collected on a Sunday at the four coastal stations of Tynemouth, Cullercoats, Whitley Bay and Monkseaton. On one glorious Sunday in 1938 a maximum of almost 47,000 was reached, while a June Sunday in 1937 which was also a race day brought more than 56,000. A record figure for a bank holiday was reached on Whit Monday in 1933 with well over 95,000, but this was exceeded on August bank holiday 1939 with 100,000. For those making the journey from Newcastle the return fare was 1s (5p), available by any of the three routes to any of the four coastal stations.

More complication arose from the unequal loadings. While the outward traffic would be spread over the whole morning and well into the afternoon, the return traffic was likely to be concentrated into a period of only two hours or so in the evening when everyone wanted to travel home. And the weather could be an extra joker in the pack; if rain set in during the afternoon, the homeward rush would start earlier than anticipated. On the other hand, a wet start to the day could mean that an expected early rush did not materialise, though if the sun smiled around midday then the crowds would suddenly appear.

To cope with such eventualities a special sub-control, established as part of the telephone traffic control introduced in the Newcastle area in 1938, was ready to take action by making such alterations to the timetable as were necessary to meet the demands of the moment, or to take emergency action in the event of a train failure or other mishap. A Sunday evening homeward rush, for example, might find Newcastle-bound trains from the northern part of the circle filling up at Whitley Bay and having no room to take on passengers waiting at Tynemouth; an outward-bound train via Wallsend might therefore be halted at Tynemouth and then reversed to bring back a crowd from this station.

Three special Sunday timetables of varying intensity were available. The choice of which one to put into operation was made on the Saturday by the District Superintendent and the District Passenger Manager, based on their own experience and knowledge of local conditions and, not least, on the weather forecast. Instructions were then sent out accordingly. Timetable A provided for about 90 departures from Central and called for the services of six six-car trains and four eight-car trains. Timetable B, which provided more than 100 departures, needed seven six-car trains and six eight-car trains. Timetable C, the most intensive, required 12 six-car trains and five eight-car trains, and also gave an extra 15 departures from Manors North.

With the electrification to South Shields, the system had attained its maximum extent. Suggestions for further extensions were made in 1949 in a report to the Ministry of Town & Country Planning on the development of railways in the northeast. The report recommended electrification of the Newcastle–Sunderland route, as well as along the Newcastle–Carlisle line, first as far as Ryton and then eventually on to Hexham to deal with commuter traffic. Among other proposals was a drastic reconstruction of Newcastle Central; a two-level layout was envisaged, with the lower level given over entirely to the augmented electric services which would be handling the expected increased suburban loads.

But not only did these visions fail to materialise, even the existing electric lines fell under a shadow. Already by the mid-1950s the Tyneside electrics were officially reported to be running at a substantial loss: where average receipts per passenger were only 6d, average direct costs were 7½d. The services were therefore put under scrutiny, and in the outcome new timetables saw the withdrawal of some lightly-loaded runs and the widening of evening headways in an

Tyneside Express: a feature of the Tyneside electric lines was the operation of various 'express' services to give rapid communication between Newcastle and the coast.

Above:
The 8.42am express from Monkseaton, via the Benton southeast curve, discharges its passengers on the up main platform at Manors East. *I. S. Carr*

Below:
The 1.03pm to Tynemouth (running non-stop from Manors North to West Monkseaton) awaits departure from Newcastle Central. Both photographs were taken in the final years of electric operation; the last electric trains on the North Tyne loop ceased on 17 June 1967. *I. S. Carr*

Above:
A wintry scene in the last days of electric operation on the Newcastle–South Shields line; a 1950-type two-car unit leaves Pelaw en route for South Shields at the end of 1962. Journey time with the replacing DMUs was increased by four minutes to 29 minutes, which did not compare too well with the 30 minutes offered by Northern General's recently established express buses. *I. S. Carr*

Right:
A contrast in twin-sets: a 1937 LNER 2-car articulated unit for the Tyneside electric lines makes an interesting comparison with its 1980s counterpart, the twin articulated Metrocar for the Tyne & Wear Metro. Although the LNER set retains the traditional railway coach outline, it diverges from the conventional in the open saloon layout with large windows and end doors, as well as in the articulation (although by this time this was an established practice with LNER coaching stock). The Metrocar reflects the styling of a later age, and apart from its lighter construction, it incorporates a more even door distribution to speed loading and unloading. The principle of articulation is retained, but the two individual cars of the unit are treated more as one entity. And of course third rail current collection has been replaced by overhead. Both units were built by Metropolitan-Cammell. Note also the continuance of a two-tone livery, while changing art styles are represented by the LNER totem and the Tyne & Wear logo.
Crown Copyright, National Railway Museum, York/ Tyne & Wear PTE

attempt to reduce the loss. New rolling stock introduced on the South Shields line in 1955 seemed to give hope of a brighter future, but then the 1960s brought the complete withdrawal of electric services in the face of falling traffic, rising costs and the prospect of heavy capital expenditure for new equipment. Diesel multiple-units took over the South Shields line in 1963 (by which time the number of passengers had dropped to half the 1938 level) and the north Tyne in 1967. But this was not to be the end of the story, for the 1970s brought the turn of events which led to the resurrection of much of the system in the form of our Metro of today.

'I am a thorough believer in the value of a well-regulated monopoly', the NER's general manager George Gibb had stated in the early years of the century. 'Monopoly secures harmonious, consistent and well-ordered progress'. As far as the North Eastern was concerned, few challenged his contention. Within its own area, the NER had a virtual monopoly of rail transport, yet at the same time this had not produced the evils that many people proclaimed were the inevitable outcome of a monopoly; rather the NER had exercised its position to provide services which were unsurpassed by any other railway company. Gibb contended that it was impossible to point to anything of permanent value, 'either to the trade or to the travelling public, which would not have been secured, and better secured, if all districts were served, as the north-east district is served, by one railway'. The public did not benefit by competition; 'what the public benefit by is the steady utilisation of all improvements in railway working and rolling stock construction, and that can be best secured, in my judgment, under a monopoly with a free hand.'

While the NER's Tyneside electric lines were sufficient justification of Gibb's faith, the railway's monopoly did not extend to other modes of transport which developed as competitors to the railway. The installation of electric tramways provided a competitive element to stimulate the NER into electrification, and to clarify its philosophy on the role of each. Later, still more vigorous competition had arisen as the tramcar was displaced by the motorbus, which grew to challenge the railway's role in suburban and interurban transport. It remains a tribute to the strength of the railway's position that it was able to respond to the challenge, and that in the motor age the electric railway still had a crucial part to play in the overall transport pattern. This was no less forcibly demonstrated by the creation of the Tyne & Wear Metro under the exacting conditions of the 1970s. Some 70 years after the NER had taken the step towards the establishment of an electric rapid transit system, the basic principles remained no less valid. Granted that in the age of the private motorcar, no operator could enjoy a real monopoly in transport, Gibb's words might well have been recalled in the operations of the new Passenger Transport Executive, which had the power to use its virtual monopoly position within its area to develop a transport system incorporating both the established rail principle and the motorbus, not in competition, but as an integrated whole. Can we doubt that Gibb would have approved?

13 The Changing Scene at Central

This week an English Electric 2000hp Type 4 diesel-electric locomotive has been used for passenger haulage on the East Coast main line between Kings Cross and Newcastle.
Railway Gazette, 29 August 1958

While successive generations of spotters at Newcastle Central would record an ever-changing panorama over the years, the older ones of us who had outwardly put away such childish things, still glanced enviously and recalled that trains were not what they used to be. Of course, our own spotting days remain fixed and immutable as a snapshot of the scene at that time; dare we return in reality and find it all changed? The big Atlantics and the 4-4-0s of the early years of the century were giving way in the 1920s and 1930s to the great Pacifics – though not without a strong rearguard action by many of the older locomotives still showing their paces. In the early 1920s came the realisation that the North Eastern as a separate concern was no more, although the name was basically the same, with just a 'London' added to it: the old provincial NER had gone forward and conquered the metropolis! Engines were still bright green, and if the old North Eastern crimson coaches gave way to brown, varnished teak had long been familiar on the East Coast Joint Stock.

The final flourish of NER motive power just as the grouping took effect was the Raven Pacific. If we had been in the right place at the right time in the spring of 1923 we could have seen a giant of a locomotive, still in its works grey and coupled to a dynamometer car, set off on a trial run to Edinburgh. This was No 2400, the first of a select class of five engines which looked like elongated versions of the celebrated Atlantics whose heaviest duties they were designed to take over. The quintet were shedded at Gateshead and later received names of cities, No 2400 becoming *City of Newcastle.* If they were not destined to achieve the fame or longevity of the more numerous Gresley Pacifics of Great Northern pattern, not for worlds would any true North Eastern enthusiast have conceded that the 'Cities' could have been inferior to anybody else's engines. *City of Newcastle* itself took part in the Stockton & Darlington Railway centenary procession to exemplify modern locomotive practice, and what more worthy accolade could we want?

Nevertheless, from the 1920s on it was the Gresley Pacifics that dominated the main East Coast expresses, steaming in and out of Central with the increasing loads of the fastest trains. At Gateshead sheds around the mid 1920s, not only the native Pacifics were on hand, but newcomers from the Gresley stables. Prowling around the sheds we might have spotted such romantic (and sometimes mysterious and improbable) names as *Sceptre, Sunstar, Gladiateur, Tranquil, Harvester, Isinglass, Galopin, The White Knight, Night Hawk, St Galien* or *St Frusquin*. At Heaton we might have noted *Bayardo* or *Shotover, Dick Turpin* or *Neil Gow.*

New train sets were provided in 1924 for 'The Flying Scotsman', now the official title for the renowned 10am from Kings Cross. Typically it comprised 11 coaches; in the middle was the appropriate centre-piece, the 'triplet' dining car set, a three-coach articulated unit consisting of third-class and first-class restaurant cars with kitchen car between. By the time we see the train pull into Newcastle just after half past three, this unit has already served three sittings for lunch and is getting ready to serve afternoon teas on the rest of the journey northwards.

On the afternoon of Monday, 11 July 1927, a crowd of eminent local worthies, railway enthusiasts and curious spectators thronged the platforms of Central to cheer the arrival of *Flying Fox* and its train on the inauguration of the first non-stop service between London and Newcastle, at the time the longest non-stop run in the world. When the train pulled up at 3.20 senior railway officers presented driver and fireman with telegrams of congratulation from the LNER's chief general manager Sir Ralph Wedgewood, the Mayor of Newcastle presented them with pipes and cigars, and local businessmen offered their own congratulations on this new high-speed commercial link with the metropolis. The train, which was the first part of the 'Flying Scotsman', had left Kings Cross at 9.50, also with due ceremony. The non-stop service continued to run four days a week throughout that summer. Of the seven Pacifics specially allocated to its working, four were Gateshead inhabitants: *Gladiateur, Harvester, Galopin* and *The White Knight.*

More was to come, for in 1928 the 'Flying Scotsman' was booked to run without a stop from Kings Cross to Edinburgh, setting a new record for the longest non-stop run in the world. The first such journey was made on Tuesday, 1 May, and again the platforms at Newcastle Central were crowded to witness what was probably the first occasion a scheduled passenger

Above:
Long a stalwart of the East Coast main line through Newcastle, LNER 'D20' class 4-4-0 No 2109 (ex-NER Class R, built in 1901) works a local including characteristic NER stock in this scene from the summer of 1938. *Real Photographs*

Pacific power.

Below:
The last locomotives produced by Raven for the NER were five Pacifics, the first of which (No 2400 here) appeared in 1922. 'Massive machines' (as Cecil J. Allen describes them) they had three cylinders, 6ft 8in coupled wheels and 200lb boiler pressure, the locomotive alone weighing nearly 100 tons. All five were stationed at Gateshead for the East Coast expresses; they received names in 1924–5, when No 2400 became *City of Newcastle. Ian Allan Library*

Above:
East Coast motive power in LNER days was dominated by the Gresley Pacifics, and among those shedded at Heaton was No 2576 *The White King;* the Westinghouse pump fitted to locomotives for service in the North East area is a prominent item.
Ian Allan Library

Below:
The age of speed: Newcastle to London in four hours by the LNER's streamlined 'Silver Jubilee' train introduced in 1935 and seen here hauled by Pacific No. 2510 *Silver Link. Real Photographs*

train had run through the station without making a stop. The 'Scotsman' from Edinburgh came through at 12.40, while its opposite number from London steamed through on platform 8 at 3.22 in the afternoon. It was again splendid publicity, even if it did cast more than a sidelong glance at the traditional opposition on the West Coast route.

The non-stop 'Scotsman' ran in summer only, and the more normal trains retained sensible stops at such important places as Newcastle. Nevertheless, speeds generally were increasing at last: in 1932 the long established 8¼ hour London–Edinburgh schedule was cut to 7hr 50min, and by the late 1930s this was down to 7hr 20min.

To many enthusiasts the most memorable day in King George V's Silver Jubilee year of 1935 was probably 30 September when at Central we saw a revolutionary new train in shining silver-grey, headed by a locomotive of modernistic shape: No 2509, named *Silver Link,* had a wedge-shaped front and a streamlined casing covering boiler, motion and wheels. In time we would become used to the shape of the 'A4' Pacifics, but the initial shock had first to be overcome. The new train was the 'Silver Jubilee', Britain's first fully-streamlined train. At 10 in the morning it started off from Newcastle Central for an unprecedented dash to London in only four hours, a whole hour faster than the previous best train. After arriving at Kings Cross at 2pm, it set off northwards again at 5.30, to reach Newcastle at 9.30. The only intermediate stop was at Darlington. Overall average speed for the whole journey was just over 67mph, the fastest in Britain for a journey of more than 200 miles. A trial run made on 5 March 1935 between Kings Cross and Newcastle by non-streamlined Pacific *Papyrus* in only 3hr 57min showed what could be done.

Silver Link at first maintained the service alone, but it was soon joined by three similar companions, *Quicksilver, Silver King* and *Silver Fox,* completing 'a quartet of strange looking monsters' in the view of that doyen of locomotive observers, J. N. Maskelyne. The original 'Silver Jubilee' train consisted of seven coaches, comprising a 'triplet' restaurant car set, flanked by two articulated 'twins', providing seats for a total of 198 passengers, of whom 78 were first class. A supplementary fare of 5s (25p) was charged first class and 3s (15p) third class, but so popular was the train that we would be lucky to get on. Its publicity value was considerable; posters carried a striking portrayal of the train, and proclaimed 'The Silver Jubilee, Britain's First Streamline Train, Newcastle and London in 4 hours; Average throughout 67.08 miles per hour'. An incidental benefit to the LNER was a substantial increase in the sale of platform tickets at stations such as Central where enthusiasts and members of the general public turned up for a sight of this revolutionary streamliner and its lucky passengers in their air-conditioned comfort.

As British Railways was to discover in more recent years, 'speed pays', and the first LNER streamlined train was followed in the Coronation year of 1937 by the appropriately named 'Coronation', which made the longer journey between London and Edinburgh in only six hours. A stop was made at York on the way down, but oddly enough while the up train also stopped at Newcastle, the down train at first did not. However, this deficiency was soon rectified. Then indeed Newcastle did very well with its fast streamlined train service, for to the daily journeys of the 'Silver Jubilee' were now added those of the 'Coronation': after departure from Kings Cross at 4pm, it pulled in to Newcastle at 7.57, on the fastest-yet schedule between the two cities. In the up direction, the 'Coronation' from Edinburgh arrived in Newcastle at 6.30pm; three minutes later it was leaving for London, which it reached after a nonstop run, at 10.30pm.

Like its forerunner, 'Coronation' also sported a distinctive colour scheme. Five streamlined 'A4' Pacifics allocated to the service were attired in the garter blue that was to become such a familiar hue on the East Coast route, while the special nine-coach train was in two shades of blue. The last vehicle of the train was also special in its 'beaver tail' rear end; internally it was arranged as an observation car, with large end windows. From deep armchairs, which we could occupy for a small extra charge, we could get a splendid view of where we had just been.

More modest in intent, but with their own especial fascination, were the steamcars which the LNER adopted enthusiastically in the late 1920s. The more modern equivalent to the faithful autocars, the newcomers combined power unit and passenger accommodation in one unit, and also brought varieties in livery, the first vehicles donning a brown mock teak finish while a two-colour scheme was standardised. Most of the cars were of the Sentinel Cammell type, but a few were of the Clayton pattern featuring an external coal bunker over the outer pair of wheels at the powered end. After experiments in the mid-1920s, the LNER had put a number of steamcars in service in the Newcastle area by the end of the 1920s. The Ponteland branch had its autocar replaced by a Sentinel for its final period of passenger service, while we could also have seen a Sentinel puffing off to North Wylam, or a Clayton climbing up the Blackhill line.

By an imaginative stroke of inspiration the LNER bestowed names on these steamcars. Not any common names though, but names derived from the old-time stage coaches: Heaton shed, for instance, housed *Rapid* and *Comet, Wonder* and *Integrity, Royal Sailor, Wellington* and *Union.* A century earlier the railways were driving the coaches off the roads; now in the new road age of competition from the motorbus, the railway was flinging out a challenge by recalling these proud names. And anyway, was it not much more thrilling (at least to the younger traveller) to ride in *Integrity* rather than simply car No 2135? If we did not know why our vehicle should bear such an unusual

Top:
A new 'triplet' restaurant car set provided for the accelerated 'Flying Scotsman' in the 1920s; by the time we saw it on the down train at Newcastle, the busy kitchen staff were preparing to serve afternoon tea. *Real Photographs*

Above:
Missed it! At first the beaver-tailed 'Coronation' of 1937 did not deign to stop at Newcastle, but this was soon put right to add another 4hr streamliner schedule between Newcastle and London.
Real Photographs

Local power: the LNER made extensive use of steam cars for short-distance services, including several in the Newcastle area.

Top right:
The coupled wheels and external coal bunker were distinctive features of the Clayton cars. No 41, dating from 1927 and still in its brown livery, here prepares to leave Lintz Green on the Derwent Valley line. It later became No 2121 *Pilot* and was withdrawn in 1936.
Ian Allan Library

Below:
Sentinel car No 2135 *Integrity* departs from Newcastle Central on the North Wylam service in 1936. *Photomatic*

41
L N E R

L N E R
INTEGRITY

Gresley motive power on Newcastle trains.

Above:
The 4-4-0 tradition was maintained by the LNER 'D49' three-cylinder 'Shire' class of the late 1920s, employed on such duties as the Newcastle–Liverpool expresses. This is No 234 *Yorkshire* on a heavy train including an ex-NER straight-sided saloon and a 12-wheel restaurant car. *Ian Allan Library*

Right:
Awaiting departure from the west end of Newcastle Central in 1936, LNER 'V1' class 2-6-2T No 481, only a year old, heads a train of elderly ex-NER stock, including a brake-end with bird-cage lookout. Some two-dozen 'V1' (and later 'V3') locomotives were allocated to Tyneside sheds, where many continued to serve until the 1960s. *Photomatic*

Below right:
Over the famous crossings at the east end of Newcastle Central a 'V1' class 2-6-2T brings in a train composed mostly of ex-NER clerestory stock from the High Level bridge, while on the far left a north side electric train approaches. *Ian Allan Library*

At Newcastle Central in the last days of the LNER.

Above:
Local trains in the terminal lines at the east end of the station. At platform 5 on the left is Class A8 ex-NER 4-6-2T No 2154, while at platform 4 on the right is 'V1' 2-6-2T No 497. Note the guarded conductor rails for the electric trains which also used these platforms.
C. R. L. Coles

Below:
A former greyhound of the East Coast expresses, an ex-NER Atlantic performs humbler duties in its later days; Class C6 No 700 (an NER Class V1 of 1910) leaves with a Sunderland train of ex-NER coaches shortly before its withdrawal in 1946.
C. R. L Coles

784

1711

Variety in motive power seen at Gateshead on a summer day in 1946.

Left:
Still in its rather faded prewar green livery, 'C6' class 4-4-2 No 784 of 1914 vintage, dreams of its racing days as one of the NER's Class V Atlantics.

Below left:
Accustomed to more humble duties, 'N10' class 0-6-2T No 1711 originated in 1902 as a member of the NER's 'U' Class.

Above:
Still only a few months old and the LNER's first new-design postwar locomotive, 'L1' class 2-6-4T No 9000 in its new green livery prepares to take up its duties. It was still undergoing trials on different sections of the LNER, its northeastern runs including work on the Newcastle–Carlisle route.
Ian Allan Library

Below:
Newcastle Central in 1949: the Pacific-hauled Pullman 'Queen of Scots' halts on its run from Edinburgh to London via Leeds. This all-Pullman train was withdrawn in 1964. *Ian Allan Library*

name, within the saloon we found a panel illustrating the old stage coach of this title and telling us of its achievements in those far-off romantic days. If romance did not appeal, then just remember that the cars were using good home-produced English coal!

Although running costs were reportedly only half those of the autocars, the steamcars proved to be heavy on maintenance, while their carrying capacity was limited, a feature common to any such units. Nevertheless they did good work on local and branch services at a time when these were under attack from the road, and the last of them survived until the late 1940s.

The LNER also brought other new motive power to our area with its standard locomotives displacing the familiar North Eastern stalwarts. On the Newcastle–Carlisle line, varieties of motive power were to be seen over the years; for a while during the 1920s we were still able to witness the running of 'foreigners' from the former North British in the shape of 'Scott' class 4-4-0s bearing such noble names as *Laird o' Monkburns* or even *Sir Walter Scott* himself, then came newer 4-4-0s of Gresley's 'Shire' and 'Hunt' classes. There were big new tank engines too; the 'V1' and 'V3' 2-6-2Ts proved their powers of speed and endurance on this 60-mile run, a long haul for a tank maybe, but this was nothing novel on North Eastern territory, and the newcomers also took their place on the speedy Newcastle–Middlesbrough trains. Notwithstanding, in the 1930s the old NER 'O' class 0-4-4 tanks, now LNER Class G5, were still going strong on the Newcastle–Hexham local service, together with the handsome 4-4-4Ts, as well as on other local lines.

New corridor trains were put on to Newcastle–Carlisle in 1936; as we recalled, the NER had never been too lavish in its provision of corridor stock, but the new coaches were of the latest design, even with arm-rests in the third-class compartments and the unheard-of amenity of a buffet car – truly this line had come into its own as an 'express' route. Speeds were improved too; the 1938 timetable showed a non-stop train timed to make the journey in only 77 minutes, good going compared with an earlier best time of 90 minutes. Similar up-to-date stock appeared on the Newcastle–Sunderland–Middlesbrough service in 1937, the typical six-coach train again including a buffet car and sometimes augmented by an additional coach or two at busy periods; the work was none too easy for the ageing NER types or even for the Great Central-style 4-6-2 tanks the LNER had drafted in, and here the newer 2-6-2 tanks were useful recruits to the motive power department.

An outbreak of Pullman opulence in early LNER days brought the umber-and-cream luxury trains into Newcastle under such titles as the 'Harrogate Pullman' or the 'Queen of Scots'. The summer of 1923 witnessed the advent of the 'Harrogate Pullman', due out of Newcastle at 9.20 in the morning and travelling by way of Harrogate and Leeds to reach Kings Cross at 3.15. The return working from London pulled into Newcastle at 5pm. The service was subsequently extended northward to Edinburgh as the 'Harrogate and Edinburgh Pullman', and in 1928 it became the 'Queen of Scots' with a brand new set of seven Pullmans. For some years to come we could still expect to see the 'Queen of Scots' behind an ex-North Eastern Atlantic as it pulled into Central over the great crossings or headed away southwards towards Darlington.

The years of World War 2 meant slower trains, longer and overcrowded, and the constant nagging question 'Is your journey really necessary?' The high-speed fliers were banished, and East Coast expresses lengthened to fantastic extremes. Streamlined 'A4s' manfully stayed the course, though their valances were cut away to expose the 'works' and they acquired an austere black livery in place of the silver, green or blue. After the end of the war in 1945 it was heartening to learn that the LNER proposed to restore its bright green livery, not only to major passenger classes but throughout its locomotive stock, though the stream-liners were to be restored to blue. A pleasant foretaste of things to come was the appearance at Newcastle Central of 0-6-0T No 8680 in the full glory of lined-out green. Soon after were to come shades of British Railways blue and green.

Streamlined fliers such as the 'Silver Jubilee' never again graced the tracks of Central. However, in the summer of 1948 the 'Flying Scotsman' resumed its non-stop London–Edinburgh run, and the 'Queen of Scots' was back in the same year together with the new 'Tees-Tyne Pullman', disappointingly taking 5¼ hours for the London–Newcastle journey against the 'Silver Jubilee's' four hours. In 1949 another train was the 'Northumbrian'. By the start of the 1950s signs of the times included the withdrawal of the last of the North Eastern Atlantics, and the arrival at Gateshead and Heaton sheds of new 'A1' class Pacifics: we shall just be in time to note 60132, 60135, 60137, 60142, 60145, 60147, 60150, 60151, 60154, 60155 . . .

A reminder of what we were seeing at this period is given us by ace railway photographer H. Gordon Tidey, writing in *Meccano Magazine* of his 1949 visit to the area. Pacifics abounded then, of course; 'Flying Scotsman' went through behind new unnamed 'A1' No 60124 and the 'Capitals Limited' with streamlined 'A4' *Walter Wigham.* The 'Norseman' from Tyne Commission Quay was in charge of 'A2' No 60538 *Velocity,* while an express goods was headed by 'A4' No 60023 *Golden Eagle.* A Leeds–Glasgow express made a colourful sight with coaches in the experimental 'plum and spilt milk' livery and 'A3' *Gainsborough* in blue. Former North Eastern locomotives were happily still about in plenty, including 0-6-0s, 4-6-0s and 4-6-2Ts. On the Carlisle line, most trains were in the hands of 'B1' class 4-6-0s, but there was also the occasional 4-4-0 of either North Eastern or

Left:
Nocturne at Newcastle: Class A4 Pacific No 60019 *Bittern* pauses at Central with an 'A4' Preservation Society special from Edinburgh to Leeds in 1966. For many years the 'A4s' were synonymous with the East Coast expresses and *Bittern* was the last of the class in BR regular scheduled service. *M. Dunnett*

Below left:
In the last days of steam power on the Middlesbrough–Newcastle service, ex-LMS 2-6-4T No 42073 (carrying express train headlamps) on its way to Newcastle passes Seaburn in 1955, shortly before the service was taken over by diesel multiple-units. Seaburn station was opened in 1937 to serve new housing as well as pleasure traffic to the seaside. *W. A. Camwell*

Below:
Newcastle for Norway: with passengers from the Norwegian steamer, Class 46 diesel No 170 awaits departure from Tyne Commission Quay with a train to Newcastle including through coaches to London in 1969. Tyne Commission Quay was opened in 1925 to cater for the Norwegian steamer traffic; a named boat train 'The Norseman' conveyed passengers to and from London. The last train to the quay ran on 2 May 1970. *I. S. Carr*

North British origin. Among the tanks were the Gresley 2-6-2Ts as well as some older NER types.

At this time steam seemed to be going on for ever as an integral part of the railway scene. We had heard that the LNER had had plans to 'dieselise' the East Coast main line, but it was to be years yet before the famous Pacifics succumbed under the onslaught of diesel power. The coming of such impressive machines as the 'Deltics' and eventually the High Speed Trains, proved that the railway heritage so strong in Tyne & Wear was no less a part of the future than of the past.

Below:
Steam, diesel and electric at Newcastle Central; the crossovers at the east end of the station fix the location in this 1963 view. Class V3 2-6-2T No 67646 enters with empty stock for a Birmingham express, an electric train leaves on the North Tyne loop, and a diesel shunter goes about its duties. Neither steam nor electric were to last much longer.
M. Dunnett

14 Towards the PTE

I have long held the opinion that local services should be for local authorities.
Charles A. Hopkins, General Manager,
Sunderland Corporation Tramways & Motors, 1939

'The Tyne district is threatened with invasion by an electric tube railway', *The Railway Magazine* warned in 1909. Since the project put forward by private promoters was of a 'speculative character', we were told, they were seeking the financial backing of the local authorities, and this did not look likely to be forthcoming. Termini of the new 'tube' were to have been at North Shields and South Shields respectively, and gradients as steep as 1 in 20 would have taken the line under the river in almost a straight line. On the standard gauge single track, a three-car train seating 150 passengers was to shuttle back and forth. Since the ferries between the two towns were carrying more than five million passengers a year, the railway might have expected ample patronage by offering a faster journey unimpaired by weather conditions. To finance the project the corporations of Tynemouth and South Shields were asked to guarantee 4% a year on the proposed £100,000 debenture stock, but the 'threatened' tube never materialised. A persistent variant of the scheme was the tunnel monorail proposed by Chalmers Kearney; on gradients as fearsome as 1 in 7 the car would have reached speeds of up to 60mph on its brief underwater journey.

The absence of any bridge downriver from Newcastle lent importance to the provision of several ferry services across the Tyne. Connections between North Shields and South Shields were maintained by the North & South Shields Ferry Co until 1863, when they were acquired by the Tyne Improvement Commission which then took over the obligation to provide services including the Market Place ferry, the direct ferry and the Whitehill Point ferry. While all three of these carried passengers, the Market Place ferry also conveyed vehicles. If we had arrived here during the early years of our period, we might have sampled the two new passenger boats which the Commission had just put into operation; each could carry more than 500 passengers and attain a speed of 11kt, and between them they maintained a 10min service. Two older boats were retained for the vehicular traffic, and they kept up a 15min service. Between Jarrow and Howden a free ferry was operated by the local authorities of Wallsend and Jarrow, in association with the Northumberland and Durham County Councils, while Mid-Tyne Ferries' service connecting Hebburn, Wallsend and Walker provided a convenient link for workers at the various shipyards and engineering works along the river banks.

Tunnels of various kinds had been advocated for many years. The historian of Tyneside's transport, George Hearse, traces the first suggestion for a tunnel between North Shields and South Shields as far back as 1798, while other advocates over the years supported a project for a bridge; perhaps the most elaborate scheme envisaged a transporter bridge which would have incorporated tracks to carry tramcars between South Shields and Tynemouth. During the lean years of the 1930s there were thoughts that a tunnel between these two towns might be built with government aid at a cost of about £1½ million as a boost to the economy of one of Britain's depressed areas, while other plans at this period foresaw the construction of a £1 million bridge at St Anthonys.

It was not until 1951 that the long-awaited pedestrian and cycle tunnels between Jarrow and Howden were opened. Subsequently the ferry was modified to take vehicles only, and in the same year falling demand led the Tyne Improvement Commission to withdraw Sunday service on its Whitehill Point ferry as a prelude to its complete cessation. In 1954 the Commission withdrew the direct North Shields–South Shields ferry, which by this time was reported to be carrying no more than half a dozen passengers on each crossing. Meanwhile local authorities were still pressing for the construction of the vehicular tunnel; intensifying congestion over the Newcastle bridges, it was emphasised, made the provision of a new north-south vehicle route a matter of increasing urgency.

As the 1950s dawned, the start of construction of the vehicle tunnel was still being delayed by 'financial stringency', though the plans were ready for the go-ahead and the necessary land had been acquired for the approach roads on either side. Some £1million had already been spent on the completed pedestrian and cycle tunnels as well as on this preliminary work; it was estimated that the new tunnel itself would cost around £10million. Moreover the County Development Plan proposed that additional link roads should be built at a further cost of about £2½million; these would provide connections with the Great North Road to take through traffic clear of Newcastle and Gateshead, and would enable traffic to and from Teesside to by-pass Sunderland. On the western side of Newcastle further relief was proposed by means of a bypass making a crossing of the Tyne over a new bridge at Scotswood.

The urgency of the traffic problem was underlined by almost 50,000 vehicles passing across the Newcastle bridges every day. Of this total, about half used the

Together – yet still too far apart?

Right:
The linking of tracks across the Tyne bridges during the 1920s made possible the operation of through tramcar services between Newcastle and Gateshead in a step towards the integration of Tyneside transport. Keeping their distance at Newcastle's Haymarket terminus are cars of Newcastle Corporation (behind) and Gateshead & District Tramways on through routes. The question of tramway replacement showed that the viewpoints of the two operators were not always identical. *R. Brook*

Below right:
Tramcars en masse: balcony-top double-deckers of Gateshead & District on parade at the depot. At their peak the Gateshead cars were carrying more than 25 million passengers a year.

Below:
Sunderland's sleeper-track tramway extension along the centre strip of dual-carriageway Durham Road was not completed until 1949 and was the last new addition to the tracks. At the terminus stands No 26, one of the Corporation's end-entrance cars of 1935, with an ex-Ilford car behind. The last Sunderland trams ran on 1 october 1954, so ending the tramway era in Tyne & Wear.

newest, the Tyne bridge, the only one to pose no weight restrictions; of the others, the High Level was limited to nine tons and was now officially designated an ancient monument, and the swing bridge which dated from 1876 had a limit of 10 tons. The Redheugh bridge, reconstructed around the turn of the century and in private hands until it was municipalised in 1937, could take loads of no more than seven tons. The nearest relief westward, at Scotswood, had been strengthened in the early 1930s but still was restricted to 10-ton loads, was unable to take double-deck buses and had lately been hampered by a speed restriction of 5mph. A new bridge at Scotswood had been planned as early as 1935, but it was not completed until 1967. Down river the only vehicle crossings were by the Jarrow and Shields ferries, which were not only constrained in the loads they could carry, but were liable to cause delays to vehicles waiting to cross, to say nothing of lengthy detours that might be necessary to reach them. And of course the concentration of bridges not only concentrated the traffic on to these few points but also forced all through traffic to traverse the densely built-up areas of Newcastle and Gateshead, with consequent congestion and delay.

Improvement of the Great North Road had been an ongoing process. Back in the 1920s Newcastle had spent some £100,000 on reconstructing its own section in order to meet the growing weight of motor traffic. The work had involved the widening of the road from the city and through Gosforth, together with the renewal of the tramway. The corporation had carried out the task without interrupting the flow of tramcars by the use of temporary tracks, for at the same time the old centre poles – now seen as a danger and a hindrance to motor vehicles – were replaced by side poles and span wires, while the two tracks were correspondingly relaid closer together, 'thereby offering greater freedom and traffic movement, minimising the danger of accidents, and giving increased effective width to the carriageway', as the City Engineer explained. The need was pressing; in 1924 Durham's County Surveyor was reporting that the total weight of traffic on the Great North Road between Gateshead and Durham had risen by 25% in the course of a single year.

Now, in the 1950s, the County Surveyors of Durham and Northumberland joined in urging the case for improvement by presenting a scarifying analysis of the obstacle course which made up the 10 miles of the Great North Road through Gateshead, over the Tyne and through Newcastle and Gosforth. Within an almost entirely built-up area, and hence subject to a speed limit of 30mph (though they regarded such a velocity as an unattainable ideal in the existing conditions), the highway was beset by nine intersections with traffic lights, two intersections controlled by police, 20 pedestrian crossings, some 200 road junctions, 15 entries to filling stations, 15 accesses to industrial premises, and more than 200 accesses to private garages. Particular hazards included level crossings over mineral railways, busy shopping centres and consequent parking on both sides of the carriageway, trolleybus termini (the trams had gone by this time), and fun fairs on Newcastle's Town Moor. The surveyors reported that under 'exceptionally favourable conditions' the journey could be made in about 35 minutes, and under 'reasonably favourable conditions' in about 45 minutes, but at peak times it took considerably longer. The short distance of less than a mile through the central streets of Newcastle to the Tyne Bridge took almost 20 minutes (an average of 3mph) though on one occasion they found it took no less than 45 minutes.

Newcastle's City Engineer admitted what many of us had more than suspected: 'at certain peak periods it is as fast to walk along some of the main streets in Newcastle as it is to travel in a bus or car.' Part of the problem lay in the presence of the buses themselves: in peak hours in the central area they constituted about 20% of the total number of vehicles. This fact of course took no account of the number of people being moved by the buses; indeed, the City Engineer's department conceded, the bus 'when moving is an admirable vehicle and contributes materially towards improving the easy flow of traffic in cities'. The trouble arose when the bus stopped: 'then it obstructs a traffic lane not only for the length of the bus but for a much greater distance, and there is no doubt that it thus constitutes a significant factor in street congestion'. In one of the city's principal shopping streets, where within the space of less than a quarter of a mile there were six bus stops on one side and four on the other, on one occasion it was noted there were no fewer than 20 buses within this short space, and they were occupying about 10% of the total area of the carriageway.

An above-average increase in bus traffic had been a major factor in the Tyne & Wear area's road problems. Perhaps reflecting the region's lesser affluence compared with other more favoured regions as measured by car ownership, bus loads had risen considerably above the national average; compared with 1938, the number of public service vehicles in the two counties was up by 60% in Durham and by no less than 85% in Northumberland.

Road improvements had not kept pace. Because of the area's traditional concentration on heavy industry, the transport pattern had historically been primarily dependent on railways; a close mesh of rail lines had brought with it an exceptionally large number of road level crossings and low and narrow bridges, resulting in numerous impediments to the free flow of road traffic and to the use of road transport. Although much had been done to improve matters during the interwar years (the Coast Road between Newcastle and Tynemouth, for example, had become one of the most heavily-trafficked highways in the area) the capacity of the roads was officially described as

Above:
If only the streets had stayed as clear as this we would have had few traffic problems! But it is still only 1946, and the atmosphere of wartime austerity seems to pervade the picture. On Newcastle's Shields Road, new corporation AEC Regent No 28 in the postwar version of the accustomed blue livery gives a hint of better things to come in public transport. Tram tracks still abound, and the complicated overhead for both tramcars and trolleybuses overshadows the junction. The few private cars are now vintage models (the postwar motorcar boom has not yet begun). *AEC*

On the former North Tyneside electric lines after de-electrification.

Above right:
A five-car DMU from Newcastle arrives at Walker on the Riverside line in 1973; the destination indicator shows 'Riverside'. Passenger service on the line was withdrawn on 23 July 1973. Passenger service on the North Tyne loop was withdrawn in 1978 to permit construction work on the Metro. *I. S. Carr*

Right:
The intricate patterns of Willington viaduct between Howdon and Wallsend are well depicted in this 1964 view as BR 'J27' 0-6-0 No 65842 crosses with its brake van. Metro service between Newcastle and Tynemouth via Wallsend started on 14 November 1982. *I. S. Carr*

WALKER

Above:
In the era of the big double-decker; Newcastle Corporation No 106 was one of a 1966 batch of Leyland Atlanteans with 78-seat Metropolitan-Cammell bodies. Newcastle obtained its first Atlanteans in 1960, and within four years had more than a hundred in its fleet. From 1963 their duties included trolleybus replacement. *Ian Allan Library*

Above right:
Put into service by Sunderland Corporation in 1963 was this Atkinson PM746H, the first of this make to have been supplied for passenger service for several years. The dual-doorway 45-seat Marshall body was arranged for one-man operation. During the 1960s Sunderland's bold plans included a rate-aided cheap fare system with one-man single-deckers, in a bid to encourage greater use of public transport. *Marshall*

Right:
Integration saw the merger into Tyne & Wear PTE of the long-established independent 'Economic'. Photographed in 1975 this well-loaded 47-seat Willowbrook-bodied Bedford YRQ, No 18 in the Economic fleet, pauses at Seaburn on the South Shields–Sunderland route. *I. S. Carr*

'completely inadequate'. However, that long-awaited link, the Tyne road tunnel, was eventually opened in 1967.

In Newcastle at the start of the 1960s the city's planning officer Wilfred Burns produced an ambitious development plan which combined a central motorway system with improved public transport facilities. While new motorways would take fast traffic through and around the city (and across the new Redheugh bridge), central streets would be reserved for buses only, with the object of providing better service to the shopping and business district. 'Failure to keep the public transport system as an attrative alternative to the car', Burns concluded, 'could only result in the city being faced with problems that would require enormous expenditure to solve, even if they could be solved without destroying the city's character.'

Similar concern was being expressed in the mid-1960s by Sunderland's transport manager Norman Morton: public transport 'must be given top priority over other traffic'. In his own town he reported that four out of five people still used the bus for getting to and from work. But travel by bus took about twice as long as by car, so public transport had to be made more attractive. Reserved tracks for buses would ensure their freedom from traffic delays, and would enable a speedy service to encourage the private motorist to use public transport and so lessen the demands made on road space.

Drastic measures proposed in Sunderland included a fleet of one-man-operated single-deckers with a flat fare system incorporating an attractive enticement in the shape of reduced-rate pre-purchased tokens. To keep the fare as low as possible, the scheme would be rate-aided, an echo of the old concept of the social service value of municipally-owned transport. A subsidy from the rates would allow fares to be kept at a low level to ensure continued patronage of public transport, which was the most effective user of valuable road space. 'A modest subsidy', said Morton, 'might permit substantial reductions in the huge sums of money involved in new development schemes... Pennies on the rates now may save shillings on the rates later.'

But not everyone was prepared to accept this view. Local company operators (with whose routes many of the corporation services were involved) justifiably felt aggrieved at the prospect of municipal buses undercutting their own; as they rightly pointed out, they did not have the benefit of local rates to subsidise their fares. Nor were the Traffic Commissioners sympathetic to the corporation's ideals: 'should the travelling public not pay economic fares for what it is getting?' they asked. It was a question that was to be asked many times in the coming years. Meanwhile Morton was doubtless confirmed in his view that 'in any future regional planning and development there is a strong case for a single co-ordinated transport authority.'

In the field of public transport, disharmony among neighbouring municipalities, and between municipality and company, due to conflicting interests in the same territory or in disputed borderlands, had long given point to the growing concept of some area authority which should possess overall responsibility for all the services within the whole region. True, agreement had generally been reached eventually when a clash of interest had occurred between two or more parties. And after 1930 there were the Traffic Commissioners (and behind them the Ministry of Transport) to see fair play and to reach appropriate judgments of Solomon. But how far was the existing situation more than a temporary makeshift solution to the seemingly-unquenchable clash of corporate identity and commercial enterprise? And how far was the rivalry of road and rail to continue before it could be accepted that full 'co-ordination' could be the only lasting way to survival?

The area concept was nothing new, but it was lent added impetus by the years of economic depression in the 1920s and 1930s. The 1937 report of the Royal Commission on the Tyneside area was in no doubt that unification was the only practicable answer. 'In view of the evidence given, and the need for further and better travelling facilities for the public', the Commission concluded, 'we decided that a prima facie case had been made out for the establishment of a passenger transport board'. Examining the problems inherent in the existing set-up as far as the municipal authorities were concerned, Professor Herman Finer in his *Municipal Trading* (1941) was equally decisive: 'the Tyneside area ought long ago to have been a single transport area.'

A major obstacle, as Finer saw it, had been 'the parochial outlook'. He quoted as example the first Report on the Depressed Areas; this had noted that Wallsend had opposed the introduction of Newcastle's tramcars within its boundaries in case this intrusion proved to be the thin end of the wedge towards the absorption of the borough into the city of Newcastle. He could also have quoted other instances we have already glanced at on both Tyneside and Wearside. While, as far as the municipalities were concerned, Finer conceded that the establishment of new transport areas and appropriate joint boards might have weakened their feeling of involvement, he believed that their representation on such bodies would 'adequately convey popular feeling' with regard to both services and development plans, an opinion not necessarily endorsed by the municipal authorities.

In the euphoria of the early postwar era, it looked as though some such scheme really would come into being. Under the Transport Act of 1947, the British Transport Commission representing the newly-nationalised sector of the industry (principally the railways) was given power to acquire bus undertakings. The major among these was the acquisition of the Tilling group's holdings in a number of

The Metro in action on the revived North Tyne loop.

Above:
A Metrocar arrives at Benton on 27 May 1980, the first day of trials to this station. The original station buildings are prominent. *I. S. Carr*

Below:
A Haymarket–Tynemouth two-unit train pauses at Shiremoor on a rainy August day in 1980. The simple arrangement of this new station is apparent. After the official opening of the Metro on 7 August 1980, public service began between Haymarket and Tynemouth on 11 August, and by the end of 1980 the Metro was carrying 150,000 passengers a week. *I. S. Carr*

companies, including United Automobile Services, though in fact the individual companies retained their existing names. Further than this, though, the Commission was required to review the road passenger transport industry with a view to the preparation of 'area schemes' to co-ordinate services within such areas, and the first of these was announced by the new Road Passenger Executive in 1949. The schemes were to be submitted to the Minister of Transport who would make the necessary Orders to give them statutory authority. The process was, however, a lengthy one, providing scope for a good deal of discussion, representation and objection, and the eventual outcome was that in practice no such schemes ever came into practice. Nevertheless the first one did reach the verge of actuality, and this was the Northern Area scheme which embraced a large sector of northeast England including Tyne & Wear.

This proposed that an Area Board should be set up to run the services within the area. It would have the maximum amount of responsibility for the day-to-day operation of its business, but would of course be responsible to the BTC and would be required to follow any policy directives issued to it by the BTC. Members of the Area Board would have been appointed by the Commission. In order to allow a degree of decentralisation, the area would have been divided into three operational districts, each controlled by a district manager who would in turn be responsible to the area's general manager, who in his turn would be responsible to the board. The duty laid upon the board was to promote the co-ordination of both road and rail passenger services within the area, and negotiations would be undertaken with British Railways on the rail side.

The area covered by this 1949 scheme went far beyond Tyne & Wear to encompass the whole of Northumberland and Durham and a large part of North Yorkshire. The main operator concerned was United Autombile Services, which was already under the control of the BTC, and Northern General was also in it along with other private operators. The municipal undertakings which would have been taken into the net included those of Newcastle, South Shields and Sunderland, as well as those further south including West Hartlepool, Middlesbrough, Stockton and Darlington. In all, over 200 operators large and small were to be brought into the scheme.

Objections there were in plenty. Opposition came not only from the private operators but from the municipalities. The Omnibus Passengers Protection Association, sponsored by the BET and with headquarters in Newcastle, expounded on the 'folly' of 'interfering' with the 'extremely efficient' bus and coach services of the area. In the association's view, the 'sole excuse' put forward by the BTC in support of its scheme was that co-ordination of services was capable of improvement; such an assertion, the association declared, called into question the success of the Traffic Commissioners in carrying out their duties under the Road Traffic Act of securing satisfactory co-ordination.

A measure of support for this point of view was drawn from Durham University's School of Town & Country Planning, which in its journal argued that, while it could not be claimed that the existing transport network was incapable of improvement, after the 20 years work of the licensing authority it was 'unlikely that spectacular improvements in services by way of further co-ordination can be obtained'. Moreover it believed the proposed new unit was too big; this would have involved some 4,500 vehicles over a wide area, whereas the professional view was that the optimum number which could be efficiently run by one organisation was no more than about 2,000. 'It is doubtful', the journal concluded, 'whether the possibility of greater co-ordination between road and rail passenger transport and between the road transport undertakings is sufficient to justify a major reorganisation of the road passenger transport industry in the northeast'.

Labour-controlled local authorities, which might have been expected to welcome proposals emanating from Labour government legislation aiming in the direction of the socialisation of transport, in fact were reluctant to accept that the anticipated advantages would accrue. They argued, quite logically, that municipally-owned transport undertakings such as theirs were already publicly owned, and that no corresponding benefit would be achieved by transferring them to another publicly-owned body. They believed that their own undertakings were best fitted to serve their community in the interests of passengers and ratepayers, as they had already been doing since the first years of the century. Their record, they claimed, was sufficient justification of the success of municipal enterprise. While this claim may have been accepted without dispute, it did not take cognizance of those problems which had arisen over the years between one operator and another, both municipal and company, and which had served to prompt thoughts of integration.

In spite of objections, the plan for the scheme eventually went to the Minister of Transport for approval and would have become effective if there had not been a change of government in 1951. The subsequent Transport Act of 1953, brought in by the new Conservative government, among other things repealed the requirement to produce area schemes, so that was the end of the plans. It was not until the 1970s, when the Transport Act of 1968 and the later reorganisation of local government (the Local Government Commission had recommended the grouping of Tyneside local authorities into one entity) had brought into being Tyne & Wear County and its Passenger Transport Executive, that the ideal of area co-ordination looked as though it could be achieved.

Under the terms of the 1968 Transport Act, the

Road and rail across the Tyne.

Right:
'There is a concentration of traffic from each side of the river on to the bridges between Newcastle and Gateshead. This creates serious problems in these towns in addition to the delays caused to through traffic.' So wrote the County Surveyors of Northumberland and Durham in 1954 in a plea for road improvements in their area. Of 50,000 vehicles daily crossing the bridges, nearly half were using the Tyne bridge. In this 1953 view, an experimental Northern General Saro-bodied lightweight underfloor-engined Guy Arab LUF leaves on a service to South Shields. *Ian Allan Library*

Below right:
The alternative mode: completed in 1978 the Metro bridge across the Tyne is the longest bridge on the river. By taking over much of the cross-river passenger load, the Metro was designed to alleviate road congestion and to offer the passenger a faster journey free from the delay and frustration of traffic hold-ups. The bridge was opened by the Queen on 6 November 1981 and named the Queen Elizabeth II Bridge; Metro service over the bridge to Gateshead and Heworth opened to the public on 15 November. Subsequently many bus services were altered to provide interchange with the Metro.
Tyne & Wear PTE

Below:
'Our bus routes aim at linking outlying villages with the tramways', Newcastle's transport manager said in 1920. By the 1980s the PTE's bus routes were linking suburbs to the 'super trams' of the Metro. The Wallsend interchange between Metro and bus was brought into use in 1982; here a train of two Metrocar units departs towards Newcastle while PTE Metropolitan bus No 463 on a connecting service waits below. *Tyne & Wear PTE*

Minister of Transport set up the Tyneside Passenger Transport Authority as from 1 April 1969, followed later in the same year by its executive body, the Passenger Transport Executive, to take over on 1 January 1970 the municipal transport undertakings of Newcastle, with about 400 vehicles, and South Shields with about 90. The Sunderland municipal undertaking, with nearly 200 buses, was acquired on 1 April 1973. With the reorganisation of local government, which included the creation of new Metropolitan Counties, of which Tyne & Wear was one, the county itself became the Passenger Transport Authority and took over the Passenger Transport Executive in 1974, when it was retitled as the Tyne & Wear PTE. According to the 1968 Act, the principal duty of the PTA was 'to secure or promote the provision of a properly integrated and efficent system of public passenger transport to meet the needs of that area.' For this purpose it had powers to co-operate with British Railways, the recently-created National Bus Co (representing the public sector companies including United and Northern General and its subsidiaries) and other transport interests, with regard to both road and rail services.

On the road side, a new joint body comprising members of the PTE and representatives of United and Northern General was established in 1971 for the purpose of co-ordinating the services of the former municipal undertakings and the companies. On the rail side, the PTAs had been given powers to make payments to BR to keep local rail services running, and from the beginning of 1972 they assumed financial responsibility for local rail services within their respective areas.

With this responsibility, and the Tyne-Wear Plan's support for the development of a rail network, Tyneside PTE took a good hard look at its lines. Put under especial scrutiny was the North Tyne loop, once the NER's pioneer electric system but in the last few years de-electrified and now worked by diesel multiple-units. Falling traffic and revenue had not justified BR in undertaking costly re-equipment to retain electric operation, but although the service ran at a loss, traffic was still substantial and fairly evenly loaded through the day. So what should be done about it?

Consultants called in to advise examined several possible options, ranging from the retention of the existing rail service to its complete replacement by buses. All the alternatives had their disadvantages. The standard of service offered by the diesel trains was less attractive than it might have been, with speeds that compared unfavourably with the elderly electrics they had replaced; new stock with higher performance was clearly desirable. Paring-down the train service, with the aim of reducing the operating loss, was rejected as self-defeating, since a poorer service would have driven more passengers away from the trains. The major defect of the rail system was, in the words of the consultants' report, its 'lack of central area penetration'; that is, it did not bring passengers into the areas of the city they wanted to get to. The railway's city outlets were limited to Manors and Central. The existing bus network would have had to be retained to supplement the trains.

One of the more unconventional possibilities was a system of segregated busways: convert the railways to rights of way for buses only, and provide entrance and exit ramps so that the vehicles could enter the busway from suburban routes and leave it to complete their journeys into central city streets. It was an exciting prospect. But not only would the conversion have been a costly process, it would also have encountered the outstanding disadvantage apparent in most such schemes for railway conversion: the railway right of way, with its embankments and bridges, was too narrow to permit its transformation into a road of adequate width for high speeds to be attained in safety. On a north Tyne busway, the buses would have been restricted to a maximum of 40mph. In addition, serious problems would have been encountered where the route was common to other BR trains, which would presumably have required to continue using their tracks. Moreover, if the buses were to overcome the railway's 'lack of central area penetration' they would have had to leave their busway when they got into the city and then take their place in the congested central streets, so further curtailing their overall speed.

As to a complete changeover to buses running over ordinary roads, although this was a comparatively cheap alternative, it was the most labour-intensive and would have called for a substantial increase in manpower. But its most obvious defect was the absence of any form of segregated right of way; since the buses would have been confined to the public highways, they would have been restricted in speed and to subject the delays inseparable from traffic congestion.

So the most promising option came back to the retention of the rail principle, but in the more revolutionary form of a light rapid transit system, making use of high-performance electric railcars which were quickly dubbed 'supertrams'. Each vehicle would be a two-car articulated unit (shades of the 1937 electric trains) of lightweight construction, operated by one man, and capable of working in multiple unit when traffic needs demanded. The 'supertrams' would traverse the whole of the North Tyne loop (though a new curve at Manors would avoid the entry to Central and so complete the circle). There would be some additional stations, and part of the Ponteland branch would be taken over as far as Fawdon. Again, this latter part of the scheme evoked shades of the past, since the Ponteland branch had been included as part of the NER's original scheme but had in fact never been electrified and had lost its sparse passenger service as long ago as 1929; now new housing develop-

NEWCASTLE-upon-TYNE

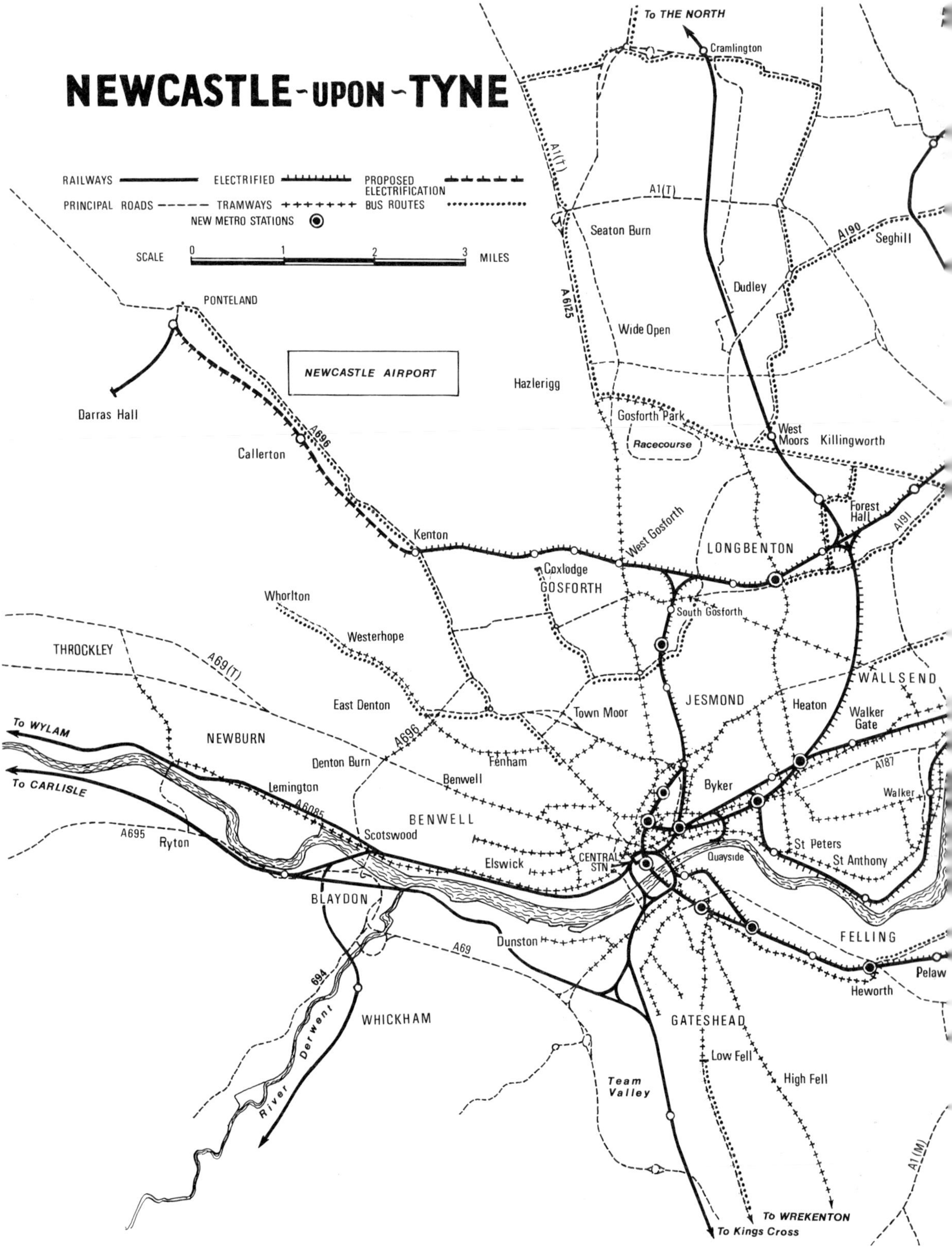